LYSISTRATA

The Clouds • The Frogs

NOTES

including
- *Life and Background*
- *List of Characters*
- *Summaries and Commentaries*
    Lysistrata
    The Birds
    The Clouds
    The Frogs
- *Suggested Essay Questions*
- *Selected Bibliography*

D0179871

by

Gary Carey, M.A.
University of Colorado

and

James L. Roberts, Ph.D.
Department of English
University of Nebraska

Cliffs Notes

INCORPORATED

LINCOLN, NEBRASKA   68501

Editor

Gary Carey, M.A.
University of Colorado

Consulting Editor

James L. Roberts, Ph.D.
Department of English
University of Nebraska

ISBN 0-8220-0776-2
© Copyright 1983
by
Cliffs Notes, Inc.
All Rights Reserved
Printed in U.S.A.

1995 Printing

Cliffs Notes, Inc.   Lincoln, Nebraska

CONTENTS

ARISTOPHANES' COMEDIES

LIFE AND BACKGROUND

A well-known American celebrity, being interviewed on TV, was asked about his singing career, and he said, "I sing mostly country-western songs because they tell it how it is." In a sense, that is what Aristophanes tried to do in his comedies: "tell it how it is." For over fifty years, the Greek stage had been dominated by superlative, but often depressing and emotional tragedies. Suddenly, Aristophanes introduced first-rate earthy, comic dramas to the Greek audiences. Theater has never been the same since. Aristophanes' comedies were radical and lasting innovations.

Aristophanes, however, was not a man whom one would label as "funny"; his plays are not filled with a series of one-liners. He was a very serious comic writer, keenly aware of his debt to earlier dramatists – in particular, to Aeschylus, the playwright often referred to today as "the father of Greek tragedy." Both Aeschylus and Aristophanes held similar viewpoints about Athens, and readers can better understand Aristophanes' comedies if they have some knowledge of the cultural context that preceded Aristophanes and if they have some knowledge of Aeschylus and other early Greek dramatists.

Aeschylus

Like Aristophanes, Aeschylus grew up in a country that was shaken almost daily by the tremors of impending war. The mighty enemy of the Persian Empire was a continual threat to Athens' peace, and young Aeschylus gained a place in history as a valiant warrior/soldier long before he attained fame as a dramatist. His name is linked forever with the crucial Battle of Marathon, and his early poetry is filled with an abundance of allusions to the painful hardships and miseries of war.

When Aeschylus finally began writing dramas, he was middle-aged, but his genius was recognized almost immediately. He wrote over eighty known plays, and at least thirteen times during his lifetime he won first prize in the Athens' drama festivals. After Aeschylus' death, according to the few records that have survived, his plays continued to win awards, and he accumulated at least thirteen additional first-place awards during their revivals.

When we speak of Western Civilization, we begin with the Greeks, and we turn to their epics and dramas to discover what Western Civilization was like in the beginning. Almost all Western world literature anthologies begin with Greek literature, usually with their epics and with the plays of Aeschylus. Remarkably, this literature is as fresh and as exciting to us today as it was to the Greeks of Aeschylus' era. Frequently critics lament the fact that only seven of Aeschylus' plays have survived intact. It is surprising, though, that these seven plays have survived. When we consider the composition of paper/papyrus itself, how ink was made, as well as the whole concept of writing down dramas and preserving them, these seven plays seem like priceless treasures – as do the few facts that we know about Aeschylus himself.

Perhaps the most important information about this early Greek playwright is not found in formal "records" – that is, his birth date or the date when he died, or the dates of his martial triumphs and his dramatic victories. The most critical keys to understanding Aeschylus lie in the plays themselves; it is there that we discover his point of view about men and women and war, about culture, and about the Greek gods – in short, how he felt about his society and his city of Athens, and about the future of the perilous Hellenic civilization. For example, had Aeschylus not been both a warrior and a poet/playwright, his dramas probably would not have reflected so intensely and clearly his belief that Athens and its culture *must* survive. But Aeschylus was clearly bent on his – and Athens' – survival. In one of Athens' most crucial battles, the naval encounter with the Persians at Salamis, Aeschylus was present. He witnessed the crushing defeat of the Persian fleet. Athens was saved forever from being absorbed into the antithetical, powerful forces of Oriental thought and principles.

Greece became an empire, and Athens' new, original "Western" thinking and creativity were hers to nurture. She did just that, and it was in her plays and epics that we have the synthesis of her unique interpretations of life – of the importance of literature, dance, theater, and art to daily living. Most of her early creativity has its roots in her literature and many of her contributions to Western civilization have their genesis in her dramas.

Aeschylus' family belonged to the aristocracy of Athens, and he believed that part of the reason why the Greek peninsula had such trouble containing and countering its enemies was because it was fragmented into so many disparate city-states and factions. In his own city-state of Athens, he saw a microcosm of the Greek nation torn by political rupture: the masses vs. the aristocracy. Remember that Aeschylus was in his forties and fifties when he wrote most of his best plays. He mistrusted young upstarts who were filled with an abundance of youthful pride and energy and new ideas about how Athens should be governed. Aeschylus was a political conservative. His values and mores had been tested by time and by war. Athens had survived because of them; they were not to be tampered with – or questioned. Aeschylus believed that Athens was heir to a high principle and purpose, something outside herself – Fate, Death, Destiny – and a person was supposed to cope with it, fear it, and revere it. New ideas involving innovation and resolutions to fate and to foreigners were heresy to him. Man, he believed, should not attempt to create new answers or solutions to life's calamities. Those physical and intellectual battles had already been fought. To give credence to too much innovation was to invite anarchy. Order was fundamental for survival.

For his *Oresteia,* Aeschylus chose a myth six or seven hundred years old and used it as a dramatic vehicle on which to hang his ideas. At the core of the trilogy is the murder of a king and the retributions that result. In the plays, Aeschylus shows that in some matters, there is no resolution. We must strive to structure some sort of order to our lives, but, ultimately, we are at the mercy of the gods, and the gods are as unpredictable as the weather. Once a citizen recognizes this fact, he should try to build a solid structure of government as well as a strong social structure, both of which will withstand foreign powers, internal strife, and hopefully, the worst of the gods' wrath. A healthy fear is necessary if man, and Athens, were to continue to survive.

In a parallel to man's framework for his civic government was a framework of underlying principles that governed each man's individual life. Fate was not always "fair," yet how one reacted and coped with the conditions that fate blessed one with, or, conversely, plagued one with, was the key to one's character. Human beings *are* responsible for their individual actions. We are at the mercy of the gods, but we must not give up. Evil exists, but man should be willing to risk committing himself in order to right existing wrongs.

At the core of all of Aeschylus' tragedies is a central character who tries to overcome life's obstacles. Usually this person fails, but he, or she, does not give up. Aeschylus celebrates the struggle, and he measures the value of a man or woman by the way in which they confront and commit themselves to the struggle. In general, it is not a physical death that is "tragic" in Greek tragedies; instead, it is something more nebulous. The fact that Oedipus murders his father and marries his mother is ultimately not as tragic as his excess of self-confidence. Oedipus is convinced that *he* cannot be responsible for his city's plague. He contains a pride that swells to such massive proportions, that when it is punctured, he is overcome. Similarly, the tragedies of both Clytemnestra and Orestes lie not in the physical murders which each character commits, but in the anguish that each of them suffers from their knowledge that they *must* commit the murder. Yet the courage that Oedipus exhibits when he physically blinds himself to a situation which he can no longer bear "to see" – and, afterward, when he commits himself to live, with the knowledge of what he has done, and a recognition of the enormity of his blind pride and self-confidence, as well as his ignorance of his impotence in a world ruled by the gods – this is the positive message that we receive from the tragedy. Oedipus' courage is paramount. It is, likewise, the courage of Clytemnestra and Orestes that we admire. Aeschylus argued that one should struggle against all curses, using the Greek concepts of reason and justice: order *must* be fought for within an accepted, moral – if not always legal – framework.

Sophocles

The next genius to dominate the Greek theater was Sophocles, a man some thirty years younger than Aeschylus. And if ever it can be said of a genius that he was blessed – in his lifetime – with good fortune, this can be said of Sophocles. His father was a wealthy merchant and their village, just outside of Athens, was a peaceful, beautiful, civilized place. Sophocles was a healthy and well-educated young man. An early attempt at playwriting was judged to be better than one written by Aeschylus, the acknowledged master of Greek drama.

The play's success was no fluke. Sophocles wrote over one hundred more dramas, and at least twenty of them won first prizes. Unlike Aeschylus, Sophocles was not obsessively political, yet Sophocles served on at least two civic and military boards of Athens. He was president of the board that collected tributes from Athens' allies. Thus, he was not a stranger to politics; indeed, he was an extremely popular public figure. He is remembered by his peers as much for his charm as he is for his dramas.

He had a salon of sorts and was fortunate enough to be born during a brilliant era, a time when he rubbed elbows with such historians as Thucydides and Herodotus, and with Pericles (Athens' leading statesman). He was also friends with such literary giants as Aeschylus and Euripides, and was a close friend of Greece's most renowned sculptor, Phidias, the artist responsible for the design of most of the Parthenon. In addition, Sophocles was good-looking, had his own boys' choir, and was a champion wrestler. He was, anachronistically, a "Renaissance man."

Dramatically, Sophocles is remembered most for his development of individual characters – particularly his women characters, such as Electra, and for Antigone, as well as many of his lesser-known heroines. He was not as conservative as Aeschylus in his attitudes toward the gods, nor are his plays as "intellectual" as those of Euripides. In contrast, Sophocles accepted the framework of the world as it was, and he began focusing on the "humanness" of his characters – but not to the extent that Euripides would do later. His Electra, for example, contains a kaleidoscope of emotions. Sophocles focuses on her deep degree of love, then hurls us into her dark capacity for hatred; we witness her daily despair, then we are drenched by her ecstasies and joys. His Antigone is a woman of instinct; her love for her brother is so great that she cannot leave him improperly buried. By coincidence, Antigone is doing "what is right" – that is, she is obeying the laws of the gods, but, foremost, Antigone is obeying a deep and fierce loyalty and love for Polynices. Antigone is *not* a religious martyr. She is a stubborn, loving sister and woman. We admire her monumental commitment to her own moral code.

The new laws of Antigone's uncle, Creon, were irrational – imposed *not* for order, but to make Creon's subjects fear him. Antigone's love for Polynices is so great that she is driven to defy a despot's edict. Her emotions dominate her reason. She will not be compromised – even if she has to lose her life. The play, then, is highly romantic. The suicide of Antigone's fiancé is really superfluous, but it is further proof that this is a play built around the power of love. The right of the state vs. individual conscience is determined, finally, by a person's commitment to love. Aeschylus was the playwright of reason and order; Sophocles spoke for the entirety of the human soul; for the most part, his major characters were heroic, at least in a moral sense.

Euripides

Euripides, the third in the trio of great Greek tragedians, spoke for the liberals and for the reformers. His major characters were emotional and very human, but were often *not* heroic – precisely because they *were* human.

In Euripides, we have a playwright who might be loosely described as a brilliant Attic beatnik. History records that he was acutely anti-social and spent a lot of time sitting in a cave, looking out at the sea, alone and lost in thought. All sorts of conflicting tales have accumulated around this enigmatic genius. The facts of these stories can only be guessed at, of course, but from his dramas, we can glean some clear truths about the playwright's inner nature. His tragedies are far different from those which preceded them.

Aeschylus, for instance, showed how man could better comprehend and cope with the realities of chaos and uncertainty by turning to myth, for example. Sophocles used myth in order to show the fullness of man's – and woman's – *human* dimension and their capacities for heroism, courage, and love. For Euripides, however, myth was, for the most part, only myth.

Euripides was neither an honored warrior/poet like Aeschylus, nor was he a good-looking, popular and brilliant social lion like Sophocles. His father yearned for an athletic son, one who would bring the family many honors; therefore, Euripides endured long years of enforced athletic training. He loathed those years, and when he was grown, he asked his father why he had been forced to spend his adolescence throwing javelins, the discus, and running. His father replied that an oracle had prophesied that Euripides would someday be a famous athlete. That finished off whatever faith Euripides may have had in oracles.

As an adult, Euripides was allegedly a melancholy, cuckolded husband, and as a result, tended to be unsociable. Yet he was a prolific playwright, writing more than ninety plays. He continued to write despite the fact that only four of his plays won prizes during his lifetime. Nineteen plays have survived, compared with fewer than ten each of Aeschylus and Sophocles. The rich diversity of his plays is evidence of his ever-fertile, ever-developing imagination and his maturity as a dramatist.

Euripides' contemporary critics were many, however, and they were very vocal. Aristophanes, for example, ridiculed him in public and onstage. Yet these criticisms did not focus so much on the *form* of these dramas as it did on the *content* of these dramas. Structurally, Euripides' tragedies are not even mildly radical; instead, it was the characters in his tragedies whom his critics objected to. Euripides exposed human frailties and portrayed cowardice and suffering and weakness in his major characters as no one had done before. Truly, *his* men and women suffer. And they die, and they are very often *not* traditionally heroic, nor are they always admirable. Often his women (Medea and Phaedra, for example) are mad – driven to their madness by love.

In addition, Euripides was a fervent pacifist, and this quality was enough to prejudice many critics and theatergoers against him. Few Athenians enjoyed seeing proof onstage that their military victors were often men who compromised their values for military victories – or that they were men who sometimes suffered great personal losses because of their military victories. This irony rankled the viewers of Euripides' plays. Yet they were drawn, irresistibly, to his plays.

Aesthetic distance was often done away with by the intensity of Euripides' plays. Even today, some people maintain that they are *too* intense. They frighten people because the audience can see the possibility of their own, until-now, unimagined suffering and madness onstage before them. The psychological insights that Euripides had for his characters are keen and abundant. A top-rate actress portraying Medea, for example, can paralyze viewers because one rarely encounters a woman onstage in a contemporary drama who is so injured and who suffers so terribly, and yet who is so passionately articulate. When she decides to slaughter her own children, her decision is incredible – we almost refuse to believe her – but we do because of Medea's capacity for passion and love and revenge.

The psychology behind Phaedra's suicide is not as dramatically overwrought as Medea's, but Phaedra's anguish is as intense as Medea's emotions. Her passions are ultimately so tangled that to unravel them is to make us fear the demons which lie hidden in our own psyches.

Perhaps Euripides suffered far more than anyone realized from his acute social rejection. Throughout his tragedies, his sympathies clearly lie with the oppressed, particularly with women and slaves. Possibly because his wives made his life so unhappy, he was able to sympathize with the great multitude of Athenian women whose husbands treated them as chattel. The key to the genesis of Euripides' characters can never be truly ascertained, but throughout his career, he continued to create masterful 'individuals' and continued to defy those who labeled him as an eccentric or a pacifist. We are richer in dramatic legacy because he chose, finally, to scoff at athletics and, instead, tried his hand at painting, and then mastered the art of writing elaborate choral odes before he finally focused his brilliance on the stage. He brought the disciplines and the stimulus of those arts to his writing, and, as a result, he brought a new theme to the world of the drama: man's inhumanity to man.

Do we wonder why Euripides was alone so often? To picture mankind and womankind as passionately as he did, and then unashamedly cry out for *all* humankind – this was unheroic to the vast majority of martial-minded Athenians. For this reason, however, Euripides is remembered as being one of the first, and certainly one of the strongest, voices of humanism. His tragedies exposed *private* tragedies, and he continued to proclaim throughout his life that patriotism should not be blindly embraced.

It is said that Euripides died in self-imposed exile. But he was not alone. He died in the close company of once-famous artists – a musician, a painter, and a historian, among others. He died enclosed by a small circle of friends who believed in the possibility that man was free. Such a message was dangerously suspect, and as long as Euripides was alive, men avoided him. After his death, however, Euripides' humanism was hailed throughout the length of Greece. His tributes are unsurpassed. "All Greece hath Euripides won" reads his epitaph. He would have loved the irony.

Comedy and Aristophanes

We cannot be absolutely sure, but it seems very likely that there were many other Athenians writing comedy when Aristophanes produced his masterpieces. There had to be. Yet the evidence is not there.

There are no other full-length examples of comedy except those of Aristophanes. Even Aristophanes, in his own work, alludes seemingly to other writers of comedy, but there is little truth that there were many other comedy writers. Four or five lines from an unknown playwright, isolated half-jokes on scraps of papyrus – and that is all. Ironically, it would be a tragic loss if we had sudden evidence that Aristophanes was *not* the best of the lot – that other, more brilliant plays have been lost forever. As it is, however, the plays that we do have from that period are all brilliant – and it seems a great stroke of fortune that we even have eleven of his comedies intact.

As with the sparse biographical facts about Aristophanes, the history of early comedy is filled with ambiguous, uncertain ingredients. Curiously, its roots seem to lie closer to the origins of drama itself than do the roots of early tragedy. For example, drama began with mime, with the re-enactment of a victory – usually a battle with other men or with a large, savage beast – or else with a large number of costumed men and women enacting traditional rites of sacrifice. This mime usually included a single dancer dressed like a ferocious animal, especially one noted for its sexual potency. There was often music throughout these rites – drums, crude string instruments, and choral-like chanting. These chants eventually developed into a kind of reciting chorus, and those people who did the mime/dancing began speaking, then declaiming, and then they became, as it were, actors.

Usually, these early rudiments of drama were performed during the first weeks of seasonal changes, those times associated with planting and harvesting. These were festival times – times of prayer for good crops, or times of thanksgiving and sacrifice for a good harvest. Filmmakers have relished in depicting these colorful and lusty, wine-soaked orgies. From all evidence, however, what we see in the movies is a pale imitation of the original excesses. There was indeed much drinking, but there was also a very serious, sacred dimension to these early, mystical, sacrificial dramas – in addition to the abundance of raucous horseplay. But the core element seems to have been the revelry. Drunken men, for example, often dressed up in goat skins because goats were noted for their sexual potency. As 'goats,' these men would loudly and unashamedly bray about their robust maleness. Oftentimes they dressed like satyrs – half-goats, half-men – singing hymns to the sexual glory of Pan and Dionysus. Fertility was important for good crops and the perpetuation of small nations. It was also important to a man's pride.

In Athens, one's manhood was measured by his sexual prowess and courage in war, and when the Athenians took time out from war to celebrate, they strutted about, proclaiming themselves to be Sexual Passion Incarnate. Artificial phalluses were strapped on and danced in, with much the same costumed abandon of "message T-shirts" worn to college bars today.

These celebrations of fertility went on for several days, and the drinking continued. There were contests to see who could tell the bawdiest jokes, who could boast the largest artificial phallus, and who could be the drunkest and still the most eloquent. Here, then, are the real roots of comedy. The Greek nation let down its heroic hair and reveled in naked emotions. They rejoiced in their folk humor, and when their masquerading and joking coalesced, soon the funniest men performed for an audience. The audience responded and before long, *they* were put onstage. A chorus was born; then it was split and placed on either side of the stage. Poets recited, the chorus responded, and, in time, the poet began narrating a story while characters were put onstage to "act out" the events being narrated. Here, drama took a giant stride forward. It had speaking parts, a narrator, and a chorus — and all these elements became the ingredients of a serious presentation because people gathered especially to see a "performance."

Five hundred years before Christ, then, people congregated in amphitheaters to see ritualized dramas as a part of their springtime Dionysian festivities.

After the early dramatists began to take themselves seriously, their themes became serious. Almost always, one could expect the drama to focus on death, and the plots of early Greek myths were usually used as the basis for the "stories" that made up the dramatic presentations. The most popular of these ancient myths usually involved a murdered father, a guilty mother, and a child instructed to wreak vengeance, either by the gods or by an inner sense of diety.

Themes of matricide, fratricide, and patricide were popular subjects, as were those of prophecy and fate, self-destruction and injustice. The actors wore heavy masks with extremely exaggerated emotions depicted on the faces. The eyes were awesomely wide-open, the foreheads were deeply creased with wrinkles, and the mouths were torn by terror or distorted by horrible distress. The drapery of the costumes was symbolic and stylized, and the actors wore special boots whose soles were built up to make the characters and their emotions appear larger-than-life. The early writers of drama wrote spellbinding "horror" dramas, and the audiences were indeed spellbound. Often-times, the same myths and characters were used over and over again, with different interpretations and results offered by different playwrights. The same chilling effect, however, was usually produced at the climax of the tragedy.

And then came Aristophanes and his biting comedies. He burst onto the dramatic scene, seemingly full-blown, his tragedy-length comedies polished, playful, and filled with a multitude of themes. He brought back the old habit of costuming people like animals and had them dancing and singing in choruses. He arrayed them in a dazzling display of human dispositions. Aristophanes also resurrected the phallic element of the old fertility rites. He padded his most caricatured "characters" – their bellies ballooned, their beards were long and hoary, and their noses and sexual organs were immense. He had the characters speaking *not* in the measured, melodious, ominous cadences of the tragedies, but in the language of common men, including the most popular obscenities of the day.

We can see how the early Athenian artists represented these early comedies on the sides of the old, broken remains of Greek pottery and vases. Obviously, the comedies and the comic characters were popular with the people. The genre became part of their common experience. It was not something hallowed and untouchable. A popular comic figure for the season was often reproduced on the dishes and mugs that the people used for daily living.

This was possible because most of Aristophanes' plays were extremely topical – that is, he wrote about the local gossip of Athens, or else took stabs at local demagogues and local issues – people or causes he didn't approve of, or like. He was especially harsh with "egg-heads" and other playwrights. Yet these "types" which he conceived were so successfully and fully realized that they evoke laughter today because the same "types" abound in today's society.

Unlike the three Athenian giants of tragedy, who used well-known plots, Aristophanes created his own plots. His comedies were always set in the present, and the characters were usually zany caricatures of Athenian citizens. The targets which Aristophanes used for his satires were many; he ridiculed the government, the gods, and even drama itself ("Shut up – over there in the wings!" and "Watch that scenery; it was painted only this morning."). His *parabases* are especially humorous, for it is here that the audience itself was addressed, and they were usually given a dressing-down. The Chorus was very often didactic, proclaiming a "message" in verbal, neon nouns and verbs to the audience. In this sense, Aristophanes' comedies are very much like today's revues – broad, satiric, full of verbal parody, political satire, and seeming to pace themselves at a reckless, breakneck speed. Pretense was scoffed at, fraud was exposed, and superstition was unmasked. Aristophanes wanted to denounce what he believed to be dangerous trends at work in Athens.

His city was used to fighting for its very life. He wanted to right the internal wrongs that festered in Athens and to show the populace what he thought was sick in their society. He sought to offer them remedies for their woes: he demanded more "manly" men and wanted old-fashioned allegience to established values. His choruses pleaded for law and order, and for government with less representation. Aristophanes was an aristocrat who denounced professional "thinkers," "ideal" utopian societies, "scientific" thought, and effeminate men. His comedies were as far removed from tragedies – in terms of their subject matter, language, and characters – as is possible. He believed that if tragedies could not furnish sufficient examples of suffering to convince men of the ruin of their ways, he hoped to convince them through comedy.

Aristophanes was a reformer and a conservative; one is hard put to find a modern-day counterpart. He used the language of a Richard Pryor to further the cause of a William F. Buckley, Jr. The combination is so unlikely that today's audiences might be caught completely off-guard by the ingenious mixture if the jokes were *all* topical. It is possible that a modern parallel to Aristophanes would not find an audience. We can enjoy his comedies because we have a historical perspective and an aesthetic distance that his audiences did not have. Aristophanes' audiences were confronted. We can enjoy contemporary comedy that is topical and raw, but we don't like it to be rude. Aristophanes was both crude and rude – and witty. We can "safely" encounter Aristophanes' comedies. For us, they are pure fun, fantasy, whimsy, satire, and bawdy buffoonery. We can "safely" rank Aristophanes' comedies at the pinnacle of the comedy genre. They do not have the majesty of tragedy, but they are every bit as effective as any of the Greek dramas. And yet, it is only by realizing the full strength of their pungent topicality for the people of Aristophanes' time that we can fully appreciate his unique, insightful genius. He stands alone as an early writer of superb comedy. He has no historical peer, and few comic writers from other literary periods can equal him.

LYSISTRATA (411 B.C.)

LIST OF CHARACTERS

Lysistrata

Lysistrata's name in Old Greek meant something like "She who disbands armies." Thus, Lysistrata is the person who conceives the plan to bring about peace to a war-torn country, and her plan for peace is simple: the women are to deny sex to their soldier-husbands until the men are so crazed for sex that they are willing to agree to any terms of peace in order to have sex again. Lysistrata is a very strong person who ultimately gains the respect of the men and women of both Athens and Sparta.

Calonice

She is the first person to show up at Lysistrata's council, and she represents the very earthy and bawdy aspects of the Athenian woman by responding mainly to sex and wine.

Myrrhine

Her name comes from the common Greek term for "vagina." Thus, in the key scene with her husband, he wants to possess her (thus, her vagina), and he is constantly frustrated in his attempts to do so. Myrrhine is extremely clever in the way that she is able to tantalize her husband while always retaining the upper hand.

Lampito, a Spartan

This is a celebrated Spartan name; Lampito is the Spartan counterpart of Lysistrata. She is a full, strong-bodied person capable of great physical exertion, but still filled with sensuality. Later, we learn that she has organized the Spartan women as successfully as Lysistrata organized the Athenian women.

Cinesias

The husband of Myrrhine. He is the only male in the comedy to be identified by name, and probably Aristophanes chose that particular name because it suggests a Greek verb meaning "to move" or "to make love," even though Cinesias does *not* do any of these things. He is the frustrated victim of his wife's clever wiles and stratagems.

SUMMARIES AND COMMENTARIES

SCENE I *(The opening scene in front of the Acropolis)*

Summary

It is early morning in Athens in front of the Acropolis. Lysistrata has summoned the women from Athens and women representatives from neighboring Sparta (to the South) and Boeotia (to the North) to meet with her. She is annoyed because none of the women has appeared – a fact which suggests their irresponsibility. Calonice then appears and inquires about the nature and importance of the meeting. She is informed in a witty interchange filled with sexual puns and innuendos that something very important needs to be done to stop the war: "Our country's fortunes are in our hands." Lysistrata feels that if the women join forces and work in unison, they can put an end to the senseless war – "then all together we will save Greece."

Calonice is skeptical. She feels that women, being inferior, can only "sit around all dolled up in silk robes, looking pretty in sheer gowns and evening slippers." Lysistrata asserts that this alluring dress code is part of her plan for peace. At this moment, other women begin to arrive, complaining about the early hour and the difficulty of getting dressed before sunrise. Some women from Sparta, led by Lampito, arrive and the Athenian women admire their physical attributes. They begin to touch the Spartans, feeling and examining their bodies and even lifting up their dresses to check under them. Finally, Lampito cries out, "You handle me like a prize steer," and the other women respond similarly.

Lysistrata then begins the meeting by inquiring about the continuous absence of the men (both husbands and lovers) and about the non-existence of sexual activity, especially since the wars have cut off all supplies of artificial sexual stimulants and equipment. If war is ever brought to an end and sexual pleasure resurrected, something drastic must be done. Lysistrata announces that the women must renounce sex altogether until the wars are ended. But on hearing this, the women do not wait to hear the remainder of Lysistrata's plan. They howl in utter consternation, saying they will "do anything rather than give up sex. . . . There's nothing like sex. . . . A woman [shouldn't] sleep alone." Lysistrata calls them to order and explains that they must dress in their sheerest gowns and make certain to be all rouged and powdered so as to get the men sexually excited. Then, when the men are all hot and bothered for sex, the women must deny them satisfaction until peace is proclaimed. (In terms of the often used, rather loose pun, the men cannot have a piece until there is peace.) Calonice wonders what the women are to do if the men, being physically stronger, *force* them to yield. Lysistrata informs them to struggle and to yield only grudgingly if the men use violence. This will lessen the men's pleasure and satisfaction.

Lampito assures the crowd that the Spartan women can persuade their men to make peace, but she doesn't trust the "Athenian rabble who have shown themselves to be so wishy-washy." She points out further that the Athenian men enjoy having their nice, well-rigged ships. But Lysistrata then reveals another aspect of her plan: the older women, under the pretense of making a sacrifice, will occupy the Acropolis and take control of the Treasury, thus denying the men any money to finance their escapades.

Lysistrata, having gained the confidence of the women, wants to ratify their agreement with an oath. They refuse to swear a oath for peace on a war shield, as men do, so they reverse the shield, fill it with wine, and each woman is suddenly anxious to swear first so she can be the first to have a drink.

Lysistrata then has a representative, Calonice, repeat the oath for all of them. This oath is one of the great comical moments in world literature: the women swear to dress sensuously, refrain from sex, and to have sex only if forced, in which case they promise to do it badly and to refuse all positions which might enhance the sexual act. Everyone takes the oath, then they begin drinking heartily. On disbanding, the Athenian women enter the Acropolis and lock the gates while the others head for their homelands.

Commentary

Even though this play is one of the world's most famous comedies, the original Greek audience objected to its serious anti-war and anti-military theme. This is understandable, however, because the play was produced in the midst of an unpopular war, and it was equally unpopular for anyone to criticize it.

In terms of the play's background, for the Greek audience, the very situation at the opening of the play was comic because women were not considered competent enough to function outside the household. What's more, they were not allowed at such places as the Olympic games on the Acropolis, the great hill in Athens upon which was built the splendid Parthenon (the Meeting House) and the Erechtheum (the House of Justice). Most importantly, women were *not* allowed near the Treasury since women, it was believed, could not possibly understand high finances. Thus, the situation becomes even more comic later when Lysistrata suggests that the state regulate its money in the same way that she budgets her household funds. Ironically, the men will find her logical approach absurd – despite their absurd wars which drain the Treasury.

Lysistrata's opening speech is a direct satiric salvo against women, and it sets the satiric tone for the rest of the comedy. Her first lines indicate that women *would* be on time if drinking, dancing, or sex were involved – but if women are asked to be on time for something serious, they probably would not bother to show up. Aristophanes thus chauvinistically asserts that most women's interests lie only in frivolous matters and that women are rarely concerned with matters of a serious nature. Throughout the comedy, Lysistrata will constantly have trouble making the women control their emotions and forcing them to seek peace.

Yet, in spite of this satire against women, the viewer or reader should be aware that it is indeed the women – and not the men – who will bring about an end to this debilitating war. It is only when the women take control that the futility and absurdity of the war is finally realized. It is this point which makes *Lysistrata* not only the first anti-war play, but perhaps the greatest anti-war play ever written.

Part of the play's greatness lies in the variety of comic devices used to present Aristophanes' ideas. In addition to the play's serious anti-war theme, these devices have become universal in any discussion of the theory of comedy.

First, there is the basic comic situation – that is, the mere situation of women usurping the Acropolis, occupying the Treasury and demanding an end to the exhausting war.

Second, in addition to the basic situation, much of the comedy is based upon incongruity and a reversal of roles. For example, women reverse roles with men by taking over the Acropolis and ordering the men to obey them. Later, Lysistrata will assert that "War shall be the concern of Women" – a concept that would be considered, in terms of comedy, an "absurd" reversal of the roles between men and women.

Third, there are the obvious satires running throughout the comedy – the anti-war satire, the satire on women and their fondness for sex and drinking, and the satire about the absurdity of oaths. Note also that throughout the play, Lysistrata's satire ranges from gentle to bitter.

Fourth, there are numerous wordplays – innuendoes, double entendres (double meanings) concerning sexual matters, plus Aristophanes' superb use of wit, sarcasm and irony – all of these are found in this scene and throughout the comedy.

Fifth, the use of slapstick or farce is first seen in the manner in which the Athenian women fondle the Spartan women. The physical dances and activities of the Spartans are pure slapstick, a lower form of comedy which requires no intellect to appreciate it.

Finally, the art of Aristophanes is that all of the comic devices blend into one another. For example, while we have the satire on oaths, we also have a satire on the childishness of men who are always making oaths and the farce of the women crowding to be the first to swear so as to start drinking. The use of the shield as a wine basin is a perfect reversal of the role of the shield.

SCENE II *(A Chorus of Old Men)*

Summary

A Chorus of Old Men enters carrying fire-pots and heavy sticks. The Leader of the Chorus encourages the men to take heart despite the heavy loads which they are carrying since they will use the wood and fire-pots to smoke out or burn up the women who have occupied the Acropolis: ". . . this rebellion shall be roasted, scorched, and burnt" because no woman can be allowed to "seize the holy image here" or to occupy the sacred shrine of the Acropolis. The men lay their logs in front of the gates and light their fires from the fire-pots, only to be almost asphyxiated by the smoke.

Meanwhile, a Chorus of Old Women enters carrying large pitchers of water. They note the doddering Old Men, staggering clumsily under the weight of the heavy sticks. They comment on the Old Men's stupidity for so blindly supporting a stupid war. Still carrying their water-filled pitchers to put out the fire, they advance toward the Old Men.

Commentary

The fire and passion of the Old Men have been consumed – they can no longer sustain a real war, so they will now stoop to fighting Old Women who have seemingly violated the premises of manhood. The men's ineptitude and advanced age are represented on the stage by all of the clumsy attempts to light their fires – and then the Old Men are almost killed by their own smoke. The comedy here is based upon the *appearance* of the Old Men. They are so old, yet they think they are still young enough to cause trouble. Thus, their total incompetence is a vivid comic contrast with the reality of the situation.

SCENE III *(The confrontation between the Old Men and the Old Women)*

Summary

The Old Men and Old Women encounter each other and, flauntingly, hurl nasty insults at one another. As the Old Men assert their masculine authority, the Old Women continue to point out the men's senility until the Old Men light their torches to attack them. The women, in turn, dump their pitchers of water (supposedly very hot water) on the Old Men, who are by then stymied by this unexpected and fierce resistance.

Commentary

In a production of this play, this short scene is hilariously comic on a farcical level. The scene would be less amusing if it were *young* women attacking *old* men, but since Aristophanes presents old, withered women attacking old, dried-up men, the comedy is greatly enlivened. Note that in spite of the witty interchanges between the Old Men and the Old Women – that is, in the wit and insults that one group launches at the other – the basic comedy lies in the farcical or slapstick action of the so-called "physical violence" between these old people – especially since we, the audience, are aware that they are *so* old that they can't really hurt one another.

SCENE IV *(The arrival of the Athenian Magistrate)*

Summary

The Magistrate arrives on the scene, sputtering forth all sorts of criticism of women, recalling in particular some of the wrong, "emotional" causes that women have embraced in the past. The Leader of the Men complains about the women's actions, but the Magistrate responds that "We men ourselves lead the women astray." He gives examples of how husbands invite "strapping young men with manly parts" to look after some of the "needs" of their wives while they (the husbands) are away on business. This invites the wives' promiscuity. As a result, the women have now cut off the Treasury just at a time when the men need money to outfit more warships. The Magistrate instructs the others to force open the gates, but he himself very carefully retires at a safe distance, out of the way of danger.

Commentary

One would have to know many obscure topical allusions to fully understand the Magistrate's speech, which is outside the scope of this commentary. However, in the examples which he cites, concerning the ways by which men unknowingly tempt their wives into adultery, Aristophanes again uses witty analogies between common terms which have a sexual connotation in addition to the literal meaning of the word. For example, the goldsmith is summoned because the wife's "fastening bolt slipped out of its hole," and this requires the goldsmith to "fit a new bolt into her hole for her." The same is true for the cobbler who is to "come and stretch it [the wife's tight sandal] a little." Aristophanes, despite his inherent aristocracy, was Greek to the core in his appreciation of life's sexual pleasures.

SCENE V *(The confrontation between Lysistrata and the women against the Magistrate and the Men)*

Summary

Lysistrata calls a halt to the forcing of the gates, maintaining that they need "good sound common-sense instead of violence." The Magistrate orders an officer to arrest her; however, as he approaches, Lysistrata threatens the officer, who then retreats in terror. As additional officers approach, more women back up Lysistrata – until the Magistrate calls for all the men to attack in unison. To reciprocate, even more women emerge and soundly beat the officers into a hurried retreat.

When the Magistrate recovers from his humiliation, he condescends to ask Lysistrata what the purpose of this revolt is. She explains that she is sealing up the Treasury in order to keep corrupt men from the monies which are used to make wars, and keep other corrupt men from using war as an excuse for stealing or profiteering. Instead, the women "will administer it" (the money) themselves. The men are shocked to think that the women would even presume to know how to handle money, because men have *always* believed that *"War shall be the concern of Men."*

Even though the women have sat silent for years and listened to all the absurd arguments in favor of war, they can no longer tolerate such blatant stupidity. When Lysistrata orders the Magistrate to keep quiet and listen to her plan, he refuses to listen to a woman so long as he is wearing the clothes of a *man.* Thereupon, the women tie him up and dress him like a woman. Then Lysistrata announces that *"War shall be the concern of Women!"*

Lysistrata explains how to end wars by using the analogy of running the affairs of the state in the same manner as housewives handle a ball of wool. Where and when the wool or war is "snarled," they, the women, will unsnarl it. Then they will wash out the wool *and* the city, plucking out and discarding all briars and scoundrels and dishonest office seekers and office holders. Next, the women will gather up all the good wool *and* the good citizens, both loyal Greek and loyal aliens, and then they will weave them into a "good stout cloak for the democracy."

The Magistrate ridicules Lysistrata's suggestions and tells her that she talks nonsense; she has never had "the slightest share" in managing wars. Lysistrata then points out the sufferings of the women when the men are away at war. After all, it is their sons, born in labor, who are killed as fodder on the battlefield. And both unwed girls and married women are left alone during wars.

When the Magistrate makes a coarse suggestion, the women overpower him and dress him up like a corpse while Lysistrata gives him a copper coin to pay his way across the River Styx, the underworld river which separates the living from the dead. The Magistrate leaves then, wearing his funeral shroud and making threats and protestations while the women retire into the Acropolis.

Commentary

Again, the comedy is based on the physical actions and, more important, upon a comic reversal of roles. Traditionally, in a physical confrontation between men and women, it is expected that the men will hold the upper hand. Here, however, the roles are reversed and the women strike terror into the hearts of the policemen. This comic technique of ridiculing a policeman is still employed successfully in modern movies and on TV. Aristophanes understood the basic human nature that would allow the audience to enjoy seeing people of authority being trampled on. The incongruity of the situation continues to be amusing even today.

The modernity of Aristophanes' play is seen in Lysistrata's view that many men encourage war so as to make a profit from it. The twentieth century (2420 years after Aristophanes) has seen too many cases of war profiteering to enumerate them in these Notes.

The scene here also shows Aristophanes utilizing the comic technique of role reversals. It is universally funny to see a man dressed as a woman (ironically, it is never, or seldom, comic for a woman to be dressed as a man). This technique is still considered comic in contemporary movies and on TV shows. On a more serious level, there is another reversal – a reversal of the dictum by Homer in the *Iliad* (Book IV, line 492) that "War shall be the concern of Men." This was an almost sacred idea that informed and permeated every aspect of Greek culture. And since Homer's time, war has always been considered "the concern of men." Consequently, Lysistrata and her women allies are violating a sacred taboo when they announce that *"War shall be the concern of Women!"*

Concerning the solution to the problems of the state – that is, handling these problems in the same manner as a housewife would handle some snarled wool – we have a situation that still puzzles many average citizens: why can't large governments run their businesses as smaller businesses or households run theirs – by balancing their budgets and other matters? The solution is so obvious that most people can't accept its simplicity.

The final comedy is again a physical comedy when the women dress up the Magistrate as a corpse and give him his fare to cross the River Styx. This implies that the authorities are *dead* to the obvious solutions.

SCENE VI *(Confrontation between the Leader and Chorus of Men and the Leader and Chorus of Women)*

Summary

The Chorus of Men comes alert as they shed their outer clothing and fear that the Spartans might be in a conspiracy with the women to defeat Athens. They decide to attack the Old Women, who then take off *their* outer garments, announcing that *they* are true and loyal citizens of Athens, and that they are tired of their wealth being squandered in useless wars. The Leader of the Women, to make her point more forcibly, strikes the Leader of the Men on his jaw with her shoe. The Old Men are outraged. They throw aside their tunics in preparation for a real "battle royal" with the Old Women. They begin seizing the Old Women, who immediately strip for battle, and ultimately the Old Women win the day.

Commentary

The absurdity of the real war is represented by the comical absurdity of the Old Men and the Old Women engaging in altercations. It is still comic for the audience to observe this ridiculous encounter, and it is consistent with the theme of the play, for the women are victorious in this encounter as they will also be victorious in ending the larger war – over the protests of the men.

SCENE VII *(Some five days later on the Acropolis)*

Summary

Lysistrata appears before the Leader of Women; she is exasperated with her comrades. When questioned about the cause of her despair, Lysistrata answers that the women are all in desperate need of sex. All of them are trying to escape by one manner or another, deserting their posts, sliding down ropes, or crawling through holes – anything to get to a man. At this moment, a woman attempts to sneak away and is immediately apprehended by Lysistrata. The deserter explains she *must* go home because her "very best wool" is being eaten up by moths, and she needs to go "lay it out" for a while. Another woman appears and says she needs to go home to "work up" her flax a bit.

A third woman claims she is pregnant, but Lysistrata pulls out a helmet from under the woman's dress and restrains her. Lysistrata then gathers them all together and explains that the oracle has proclaimed that if they, the women, hold out for a while longer, they will come out on top of the situation.

Commentary

Again, the comedy here is based upon the sexual double entendres. The woman's desire to lay out her wool is a veiled way of saying that she wants to have sex. The same is true with the other women. When Lysistrata announces that if they hold out for a while longer, the women will be "on top," she obviously means on top of the war situation. But the women immediately interpret it to mean that *they* will assume the top position in the sexual act. Thus, they agree to stay a while longer.

SCENE VIII *(Chorus of Men and Chorus of Women)*

Summary

In this short scene, the Chorus of Old Men sings a song about Melanion, a young man who disliked women so much that he went with his dog into the mountains so he would never have to see a woman's detested face again. Then one of the Old Men tries to kiss one of the Old Women. With a kick, the Old Woman rebukes him. In retaliation to the Old Men's narration, the Old Women sing a song about Timon, a man who hated men so much that he went to live in a deserted land where he befriended only women.

Commentary

This short interlude has no relevance for the modern audience. For the Greek audience which would be familiar with Greek myths and legends, these two narrations are perversions of the real stories. Actually, Melanion was extremely attracted to a young lady (Atalanta), who avoided marriage by challenging her suitors to a foot race. She always won until Melanion threw a golden apple in front of her, and when she stopped to pick it up, he passed her, thus winning the race. Thus, the Old Men recast the story to be insulting to the Old Women. Likewise, the Old Women recast their story: Timon was a famous misanthrope (see Shakespeare's *Timon of Athens*), and in the ancient myths, he hated both men and women equally.

SCENE IX *(Confrontation between Myrrhine and her husband, Cinesias)*

Summary

At the beginning of the scene, Lysistrata appears on the wall of the Acropolis and sees, off in the distance, a man who is in dreadful discomfort. Myrrhine comes forward and identifies the approaching figure as her husband, Cinesias. Lysistrata is delighted and tells Myrrhine to "roast him, rack him, fool him," but, above all, do *not* have sex with him. Lysistrata then sends Myrrhine off while she herself teases the man. Cinesias enters with an obvious erection under his toga. Lysistrata challenges him and demands that he leave. When he identifies himself as Myrrhine's husband, Lysistrata inflames his passion by telling him how much and how intimately Myrrhine has praised him. Cinesias pleads that Lysistrata call his wife, and Lysistrata wonders what's "in it" for her. He points out his huge erection, whereupon Lysistrata leaves to go call Myrrhine.

Myrrhine appears on the wall, pretending that her husband doesn't want her, as he cries out in agony. He then pinches their baby to make it cry, hoping that Myrrhine will come down. When Myrrhine does come down, Cinesias pleads with her to come home, but she responds that she will not go home until he and the other men make a truce and stop the war. Cinesias agrees and wants Myrrhine to lie down right there, but she protests that to do so would be to break her oath. After further discussion, she agrees to his proposal, saying, however, that she must first go fetch a bed because the bare ground is too hard for Cinesias.

Myrrhine returns with the bottom part of a bed, and after beginning to take off her dress, she decides that they need a covering (or mattress) to go on the bed. After giving Cinesias a quick kiss, she dashes off to fetch a mattress, despite the protests of Cinesias. Returning, she begins to take off her clothes when she suddenly remembers that they will need a pillow. Cinesias protests louder, but Myrrhine dashes back in to get a pillow which she puts under his head, and then she begins to remove her girdle, reminding him that he *must* keep his promise about ending the war. Then she suddenly realizes that they don't have a blanket, and over Cinesias' extreme frustrations and protests, she goes out and returns with a blanket, telling him to get up. He responds that he already *is* up. Suddenly, Myrrhine remembers that some perfume would make sex better and, over Cinesias' damnation of all perfumes, she returns with a flask which Cinesias rejects. Thus Myrrhine goes out to exchange it for another; she offers him this new flask, but Cinesias asserts that he has his own personal flask already up.

Myrrhine begins removing her clothes again, asking Cinesias to remember to vote for peace. When he lackadaisically says that he'll *consider* it, Myrrhine runs back into the Acropolis, leaving Cinesias in the most distressed of conditions, swearing and promising to go to a brothel.

After Myrrhine has left, the Leader of the Men sympathizes with Cinesias' distress, saying that Myrrhine is indeed vile and wanton. Immediately, the Leader of the Women speaks up in support of Myrrhine, and so Cinesias curses *her*.

Commentary

This is one of the great comic scenes in world drama and continues to be popular with audiences today. This type of humor is variously referred to as the humor of feigned excuses, or of delaying tactics, or merely as that of tantalizing. Whatever one calls it, it still brings pleasure to the beholder. The humor is based partly on our delight in seeing the clever manner in which Myrrhine is able to dupe her slow, but eager husband.

The serious theme of the play is that the women resolve to end the war by denying sex to their warrior-husbands. Consequently, in this scene we see the complete success of their strategy. Cinesias has been denied sex for so long that when he enters, he is almost bent double with sexual frustration. The "comedy of exaggeration" is seen in the fact that his erection is "as long as a spear," and thus bespeaks his torture. At the same time, the women delight in his suffering. At the beginning of the scene, they can see Cinesias' distress from afar ("He is in a dreadful state"). And from the outset, Lysistrata advises Myrrhine to tempt and torment her husband, without having sex with him—all in an attempt to end the war.

Part of the scene's humor comes from the blending of sexual double meanings with the farcical, physical movement on the stage. Recall that Cinesias' name, translated, means "to move" or "to have sexual intercourse." His name becomes even more comic when Cinesias doesn't move and doesn't have sex because his wife is constantly "moving about." And, in the final scene, when Cinesias is so intent on having sex that he momentarily forgets his vow to end the war, Myrrhine abruptly leaves him to his sexual frustration. This comic scene is proof that Lysistrata's plan for peace is indeed working.

SCENE X *(Confrontation between the Spartan Herald and the Athenian Magistrate)*

Summary

The Herald from Sparta arrives, and he too is obviously sexually aroused, and the Athenian Magistrate insists on knowing what the Herald "has" under his cloak. The Herald tries vainly to maintain that it is a "Spartan Message Staff" (a device for sending secret or important messages in a case which was shaped like a long spiral staff). When asked how the political condition is going in Sparta, the Herald says that a woman named Lampito organized all the women, who then chased all their husbands out of their beds and won't let the men touch them. The Magistrate sees this as a general conspiracy, and he sends the Herald back to Sparta to bring the Ambassadors with full powers to arrange a truce. He himself will go immediately to the Athenian council.

Commentary

This short scene serves mainly to bring about the resolution of the drama. Lysistrata's plan is finally being effected throughout all of Greece; apparently, all of the men in Greece are walking around with perpetual erections. And at the end of this scene, the magistrate sets in motion the machinery for a lasting truce to be made and signed.

The comedy in this scene is mainly bawdy and sexual. For example, when the Magistrate wonders if the Herald is a man or Priapus himself, he refers comically to the god whose grossly phallic statues were used as symbols of fertility to guard orchards and gardens. These statues were a common sight in Greece. Thus, by the Magistrate's inability to determine whether or not the Herald is a man or Priapus, he is alluding to the grossly exaggerated erection that the Herald has. It seems as though the Herald has an enormous "spear" under his cloak.

SCENE XI *(Confrontation between the Leader of Men and the Leader of Women)*

Summary

The Leader of Men tries to be rigidly stubborn and firmly refuses to be reconciled with the women until the Leader of Women helps the Old Man with his cloak and then helps him get a gnat out of his eye. Finally, the Old Man admits that he has been wrong. Then there is a reconciliation between the Old Man and the Old Woman, and the two choruses join together and sing a song of reconciliation and communion.

Commentary

Essentially, this short scene is a prologue to the next scene, where the final conflict will be resolved. The basic comedy here lies in the initial petulance of the Old Man, who is gradually won over by the ministrations of the Old Woman until the two of them are finally reconciled.

SCENE XII *(The arrival of the Spartan Ambassadors, followed by the Athenian Ambassadors, and finally by Lysistrata)*

Summary

The Spartan Ambassador arrives in a state of excitement and, after appropriate comments about *his* erection, he announces that he has come to plead for peace – any way that he can get it. The Athenian Ambassador arrives in the same sexually excited state, asserting that if they don't soon have peace he will have to seek out Cleisthenes (a well-known homosexual of the day). They acknowledge that only Lysistrata can help them, and she arrives at this moment carrying a nude female statue representing "Reconciliation." They all hail Lysistrata as "noblest of women," "a judge shrewd and subtle . . . sweet yet majestic."

Lysistrata orders the Spartan Ambassadors to be brought before her and placed on one side of her. The Athenian Ambassadors are to be placed on her other side. She addresses both groups, saying that even though she is a woman, she has a mind and a wit, both of which she developed by listening to her father and others talk. She reminds the Spartans and the Athenians that they all worship the same gods, at the same shrines – yet there are aliens in the city without such common bonds who threaten the safety of Greece. She reminds the Spartans that Athens has often come to their aid, and then she reminds the Athenians of how many times Sparta has sent help to Athens. She demands that both city-states put aside their personal quarrels and join forces against a common enemy.

The two forces take the statue of Reconciliation and, in a clever play on words, begin to demand certain portions of Greece in terms of the anatomy of the female – one side wants the "flank," another wants the "legs," etc. Lysistrata tells them not to fight over a leg or so, and by this time the men are so aroused that they agree to any terms for peace. Lysistrata triumphantly announces the pledge of peace and sends the men home to their women. This is followed by a choral song celebrating the new peace in Greece.

Commentary

This scene presents the complete success of Lysistrata's plan. During these last scenes, the men should be portrayed upon the stage as being in greater and greater physical distress because of the absence of sex. Their movements are hampered by their severe discomfort – to the point where they would agree to almost any terms of peace in order to get to their women. Ironically, the nude marble statue representing Reconciliation is a stroke of genius, because as the men look at it, they become even more excited sexually. Thus, the cold sexuality of the statue of Reconciliation does indeed help bring about the reconciliation.

Again, the basic humor of this scene derives principally from the double sexual meaning of various terms and observations. Some of them, of course, are too obscure for modern audiences. For example, when the Athenian arrives in a state of sexual arousal, he is compared with a "Herma," which was actually a fertility statue placed at the door of most Athenian homes. Its phallus was almost as big as the statue itself. Since anti-war groups had recently gone through Athens destroying the phalloi, or phalluses, it is comic that this group did not see the *live* Ambassador in his stiff, excited, sexual state. Had they seen the Magistrate, he too might have been accidentally smashed.

Finally, as always, Lysistrata is the voice of wisdom. She emphasizes that Athens and Sparta should share a common cultural heritage and join together against Greece's aliens, the true enemy. Actually, her serious speech on the status of war and the obligations of Athens and Sparta to each other offended the original Greek audience, which came to see a riotous comedy, then suddenly discovered a serious theme being preached to them by Lysistrata (or Aristophanes).

FINAL SCENE

Summary

Two Athenians emerge from inside, where the Athenians and the Spartans are finishing a banquet. The two Athenians order the choruses to get off the stage so that the Spartans will have room to come out. After the choruses leave, the two Athenians discuss what nice "charming fellows" the Spartans are. They admit that when they and their fellow Athenians are drunk, they are nice, witty people; sober, however, most Athenians aren't nice. Thus, perhaps Athenians should always be drunk.

The Spartans enter in an exhilarated state, and one (with the help of the Spartan chorus) does a song and dance routine for the benefit of the Athenians. Afterwards, Lysistrata congratulates him and announces that the men of both sides are to lead their wives home. The wives are to go with their husbands and, in the future, to avoid all such misunderstandings. She calls for more singing and dancing to end things – first, the Athenians are to sing, and then the Spartans are to see if they can "cap" the Athenian song.

Commentary

Aristophanes uses comedy to make any type of criticism. Here, for example, the drama *per se* is already resolved; thus, he uses this final scene in order to comment upon the exceptional severity of the Athenian personality – unless the Athenian is drunk. Clearly, Aristophanes was making direct fun of the audience.

As was traditional then, and is still the custom in the American musical comedy, such a play ends with singing, dancing, and a general sense of happy well-being. This is the essence of the comedy – the greatest happiness for the greatest number of people. The husbands are united with their wives, the wives are happy, there is general peace throughout the land, and Lysistrata, a woman, has been the champion of the day.

THE BIRDS (414 B.C.)

LIST OF CHARACTERS

Euelpides

An old Athenian who is tired of Athens' abundance of bureaucracy; he sets out to find a town where living is simpler and happier.

Pisthetairos

Like Euelpides, Pisthetairos is weary of the pettiness of Athens' politics and all of the distractions of daily living. He too hopes to find a utopia of sorts. He is brighter than Euelpides, and he has far more insight into the bird realm of CLOUDCUCKOOLAND. Eventually, Pisthetairos becomes "king" of the newfound "utopia."

Epops

He is the so-called Hoopoe bird. At one time, he was a man, but he had sex with his sister-in-law and, as punishment, the gods metamorphosed him into a Hoopoe bird.

Koryphaios

The leader of the birds. He is wary and even hostile, at first, about Euelpides' and Pisthetairos' idea concerning the establishment of CLOUDCUCKOOLAND as a kind of utopia, which will exist between the realm of the gods and the earth kingdom of men. Later, he becomes more enthusiastic about the concept and convinces the rest of the birds that this may be a good idea.

Prometheus

Traditionally, he is a hero in Greek dramas and legends; in this play, he displays his usual contempt for the gods.

Zeus

Ruler of the Greek gods.

Iris

Daughter of Zeus; a messenger from the gods to the birds.

SUMMARIES AND COMMENTARIES

Summary

The Birds is a comedy about feathered creatures who interact with mankind in an entertaining, instructive fashion.

Euelpides and Pisthetairos are two old Athenians who are tired of Athens' pettiness. They decide to find a new place to live where they may experience peace and happiness. Philocrates, the bird-seller, sells them a raven and a crow, claiming that these birds will lead the men to Epops – also known as the Hoopoe. Epops is a bird who was once a man, Tereus by name. This dual nature makes him something of a link between the human world and the bird world. Epops is important since he is the one who can direct Euelpides and Pisthetairos to the land of their dreams.

As the play opens, the two men and their birds arrive in a ruinous wasteland, barren with rocks and shabby bushes. They are angry at the birds for having, seemingly, misguided them. But soon they realize that they have happened upon the abode of Epops. They knock at the door, and a frightening, beaked servant suddenly appears. The two Athenians defecate in terror; then, warily, the two ask to see the Hoopoe.

Epops grants them an audience, despite his present condition of molting feathers and rumpled appearance. They relate their desire to have Epops' advice. They admire his "bird's-eye view of things and a man's knowledge of all lands under the sun." They remind him that he, like them, was once mortal:

> You once were plagued with creditors, and we're plagued now. You welshed on your debts; we welsh on our debts now. But though you were mortal once, you became a Bird and flew the circuit of the spreading earth and sea; yet both as Bird and Man, you understand.

They are excited about the Hoopoe's ability to rise above the human condition, literally and figuratively, in his new winged capacity.

Epops asks them to be specific about their intentions. They express interest in a town where the Social Register counts for absolutely nothing, where friendships are easily made and where open sexuality would be encouraged; Pisthetairos says:

> I'd like to live in a town where a friend of mine, father of a good-looking boy, would meet me and, 'You old bastard,' he'd say, 'what's this I hear about you from that son of mine? He tells me he ran into you outside the gymnasium, and though he was fresh from his bath, you didn't say anything nice to him, or kiss him, or feel his balls or his biceps – why, I thought you were a friend of the family!'

Epops tells them about such a city, down by the Red Sea, but they don't want a seaside existence. Out of curiosity, Euelpides inquires about life among the birds. Epops says it is not a bad life, perhaps because there is no *money* involved. Pisthetairos explodes with excitement, claiming to have an idea which will bring the birds much happiness. He advises them to establish a city in the sky, the terrain of the birds. The city would allow the birds to lord it over the human race "as though they were so many grasshoppers." They would form a CLOUDCUCKOOLAND in the sky; Pisthetairos explains:

> Your air is the boundary between earth and heaven. Now just as we, when we make a trip to Delphi, are required to secure a visa from the Theban government, so you, when men propose a sacrifice to heaven, can impose a boycott, refusing to transmit the smoke of their offerings and forbidding any transit through your land until the gods agree to pay you tribute.

Epops finds the idea marvelous, but he says that the other birds must accept it before they can begin work. This is a potential problem since the birds, traditionally, despise mankind.

Epops calls a meeting of the birds. They arrive gradually, wondering why the conference has been called. When they discover the purpose of it, they feel hostility toward Epops for having betrayed them; they want *nothing* to do with the two Athenian men – other than to attack their flesh and rip them apart: "death by dissection."

Epops convinces them to listen, and thus they listen to the Athenians' proposal, albeit reluctantly, and Pisthetairos and Euelpides, fearfully alarmed at the birds' hostility, do their best to speak with well-chosen words and persuasive rhetoric, trying to express their strong belief in the birds' superiority.

Pisthetairos, for example, shows them, the birds, how noble they are: they have always played an important role in earth's history and, as Pisthetairos explains, the birds are royal:

> If birds existed before the Creation, before the gods themselves, then you Birds must be heirs apparent: the royal power belongs to you.

It was the birds – not gods – who ruled over men in those glorious old days; the gods are mere upstarts and recent usurpers. Everyone knows that man has always used birds as symbols of strength and power and wisdom (e.g., the eagle, the hawk, and the owl). Surely this must mean that birds reign supreme over the human race.

By building a massive wall around the air, the birds could thereby cut off communication between man and the gods. This would force both parties to recognize the authority of the birds. If men refused to comply, then the sparrows would eat their grain and peck out the eyes of their cattle. But if men agreed to the plan, the birds would cooperate by controlling insect plagues.

Pisthetairos compares the birds' former nobility to their present state of slavery: "Now you are rejects, fools, worse than slaves, stoned in the streets by arrogant men, hunted down even in your sanctuaries." The birds hear his message and agree with him. The two Athenians propose a path to recovery. The bird Chorus asks what they should do and Pisthetairos replies: "Make the walls of brick, like Babylon." The birds are to claim their sceptre from Zeus the moment these walls are in place, and if he offers resistance, they must "proclaim a Holy War, a Great Crusade against the gods."

One sure way of punishing the gods is to slap embargoes on their lust: "no more free passage for divinities in an obvious state of erection on their way through your land to flirt with human women." Then, a bird must be sent to mankind, heralding the status of birds as kings to whom sacrifices must be made. Only the leftovers will henceforth go to the gods.

The birds wonder how they will manage money, since "men seem to set great store by money." Pisthetairos asserts that the birds will show men where great treasures lie buried in the ground. Moreover, shipwrecks will end when the birds tip men off about the weather.

Pisthetairos praises birds for their simple, unaffected lifestyle. "They [the birds] demand no marble temples intricate with golden doors. . . their highest gods live in the sanctuary of olive trees." The Athenian has persuaded the birds entirely, and the Chorus applauds him: "Swear faith to me and I will swear death to the gods," the birds say in unison.

Epops recommends quick action. It is no time for naps. He invites the two men into his nest as his guests, and Pisthetairos remembers suddenly that he is *not* a bird – he cannot fly. Epops tells him of a "useful little herb" which, when ingested, causes one to sprout wings.

The Chorus proceeds to expose the origins of the world in what is called the *parabasis* (or digression). This is the aspect of Aristophanes' comedies where he presents many of his viewpoints. Koryphaios, the leader of the birds, tells the story of creation and demonstrates how the birds are more ancient than men or the gods. The birds sing praise of their existence, of their way of life, and invite mankind to consider their condition:

> We guarantee to every single soul on earth, his sons and their posterity: health, wealth, happiness, youth, long life, laughter, peace, dancing and lots to eat! . . . Need a hideout from the law? Some cozy place to pass the time? Well, step right up, friend! We'll get you a berth with the Birds.

The Chorus appeals to the audience's sense of fantasy with its statements about having feathers, wings, and so on: "The sheer joy of it! Not having to sit those tragedies out! No getting bored. You merely flap your little wings and fly off home."

Pisthetairos and Euelpides re-enter, absurdly feathered, winged, and beaked. They begin making fun of each other; Pisthetairos tells his comrade: "*You* look like a cut-rate reproduction of an unsuccessful sketch of a goose."

They decide to name the new city CLOUDCUCKOOLAND. With that, Pisthetairos begins to supervise the construction of the wall. A priest is summoned to oversee the sacrifice. Together, they launch into a prayer devoted to a large number of birds. But the priest gets carried away with himself, inviting vultures and eagles to the feast. So Pisthetairos gets rid of him and his "portable altar" and finishes the prayer by himself.

In the meantime, however, others have heard of the great plan to build CLOUDCUCKOOLAND. A poet arrives, wishing to commemorate the city in verse. Pisthetairos whisks him away. Next, an itinerant prophet appears with a pack of worthless prophecies. He announces, as did many prophets of Aristophanes' time, several ambiguous, pointless messages. Pisthetairos disposes of him as readily as he disposed of the poet, telling him to "peddle your damned oracles somewhere else!"

Then, Meton, a surveyor, attempts to force his services on Pisthetairos, but the latter has no use for him: "I admire you. I really do. Take my advice and subdivide somewhere else." He explains that they have passed a new law in CLOUDCUCKOOLAND: all charlatans shall be whipped in the public square. This copes with Meton quite handily. Says he: "Oh, then I'd better be going."

When an Inspector comes along in order "to investigate the civic status" of CLOUDCUCKOOLAND, Pisthetairos suggests that he collect his pay and head for home. The Inspector agrees readily and concludes that he ought not to have left Athens at all. Pisthetairos delivers his pay to him: the Inspector receives a good slap in the face.

Next in the procession of fakes and charlatans is a legislator. His purpose in CLOUDCUCKOOLAND is to offer a variety of laws and statutes *for sale*. Pisthetairos pummels him with: "Get lost, you and your laws, or I'll carve mine on the skin of your tail."

As the legislator exits, the inspector re-enters, summoning Pisthetairos to stand trial on charges of assault and battery. Pisthetairos thrashes him just as the legislator returns. This see-saw continues for a while, permitting Aristophanes to make even greater fun of the so-called authorities.

At this point, the Chorus recites to the audience again in the second *parabasis*. It acknowledges the virtues and delights of being a bird and reports on the importance of birds to all of mankind. In a minor digression, the Chorus pleads its belief that *The Birds* should win the first prize for comedy in the annual drama competition held during Aristophanes' time.

A messenger arrives with the news that the wall is completed. It is beautiful, large, and stands six hundred feet tall. And only *birds* built it!

But a second messenger arrives with bad news. One of the gods has invaded the birds' air, but he adds resolutely, "He won't get away, he's somewhere around here; I feel it in my feathers." Pisthetairos organizes the forces and orders that the birds begin shooting. "Quick! Give me my bow!" The Chorus declares that it will be "war to the end, inexpressible war, god against bird."

The goddess Iris appears from above, with broad static wings and wearing a large rainbow around her head. Pisthetairos is livid with her and demands that she be arrested, much to her horror. She is here to remind mankind, on behalf of her father Zeus, that they must sacrifice to "the eternal gods." Pisthetairos retorts that the only gods *now* are the birds—that it is to the *birds alone* that man must present his gifts.

She warns him not to stir up the wrath of the gods. But Pisthetairos is not impressed or frightened: "You can inform your Zeus that if he gets in my way, I'll burn him out. As for Iris, if she dares enter into CLOUDCUCKOOLAND again, Pisthetairos promises to rape her "with his triple-prowed 'battle ship.'" He orders the slut out of his sight.

The Herald arrives from his mission with mankind. He is full of praise for Pisthetairos and asks him to accept a crown of gold, proffered in honor of his glorious wisdom. In short, the world *adores* him; he has become the darling of the mortal world as founder of CLOUD-CUCKOOLAND. Whereas men used to live a Spartan, earthy existence, they now place birds at the center of everything: "They even affect bird names. . . as for song-writing, you can't so much as buy a hearing unless you stuff your lyrics with assorted wild ducks and swallows, or doves, or geese, or maybe a few last feathers from a cast-off wing."

The Herald assures him that, soon, there will be hundreds of visitors. Thousands. Pisthetairos engineers a frantic wave of activity designed to prepare sets of wings for the expected worshippers and emigrants. The birds are pleased that men have become so enraptured of their new world.

The first arrival is a young man anxious to kill his father (Parricide). He has heard that this behavior is acceptable in CLOUD-CUCKOOLAND, but is disheartened to learn that one is also expected to care for the person who sired and raised one. He tells Pisthetairos: "Fat lot of good I've got from coming here if I have to go back home and support the old man."

Pisthetairos gets rid of Parricide by giving him black wings and a toy sword, shield, and helmet and sending him off to fight in Thrace. Then the dithyrambic poet Kinesias enters. Pisthetairos sizes him up immediately as one who needs wings. The man has no poetic sense at all; like many in his generation, he is awkward, pedantic, and a bore. Pisthetairos grants him wings and orders him to assemble a chorus of birds.

An informer arrives next, anxious to find out who is giving out wings. Pisthetairos identifies himself, prepared for a touchy moment or two with the spy. It is the informer's business to indict states with subversive activities. He is also a professional agitator of lawsuits and investigations; wings, he says, would help him practice his vicious duties. Pisthetairos is in no mood for this kind of double-crosser, so he whips the man and prevents him from obtaining wings. In frustration, Pisthetairos collects together the stack of wings and takes them inside.

Enter Prometheus, mankind's greatest ally against Zeus. He has come to warn Pisthetairos of Zeus' plans and secrets, and since he himself fears the gods' wrath, he stands under an umbrella so as not to be seen by them. He announces that "Zeus is through" – thanks to the organization of CLOUDCUCKOOLAND:

> There's not been so much as a sniff of sacred smoke coming up to us from a single human altar. I swear, we're hungrier than a Thesmophoria fast-day; and, what's worse, the damnedest lot of starving yowling gods from the back country are talking about revolt if Zeus doesn't manage to get a decent consignment of sacrificial cuts to keep us going.

Clearly Aristophanes is referring in this passage to the Athenian government of his time – a government which spent money unhesitatingly on wars, "grand causes," and frivolity. Here, men no longer worship Zeus and, in a parallel sense, citizens of Athens began to lose faith in their government.

Prometheus reports that Zeus is sending a peace mission to examine the situation in CLOUDCUCKOOLAND. He advises Pisthetairos to laugh at every offer from Zeus and his cohorts until the gods promise to restore the birds to power and give Basileia to Pisthetairos for his wife. It is she who manages the affairs of Zeus: "his" sagacity, legislation, rearmament, ideology, ultimatums, revenue officers, jurymen, etc.

Prometheus then sneaks away, back to the land of the gods. The peace delegation from Olympos arrives, including Poseidon (a powerful god who carries a trident), Herakles (as strong as a wrestler), and

Triballus (the barbarian god). Herakles wants to smash the one responsible for setting up CLOUDCUCKOOLAND (i.e., Pisthetairos), but Poseidon reminds him that they are there to discuss peace.

Pisthetairos enters and pays no attention to the gods. When Poseidon calls out, "In the name of the Divine Authority, three gods greet thee, O Man," Pisthetairos merely asks that the horseradish be passed to him. He then tells the gods emphatically that the birds will cooperate *only* if their terms are met:

> We demand restoration of our ancient sovereignty and the
> return of the sceptre to the Birds. Let Zeus accept that
> much, and I'll invite all three of you to dinner.

Pisthetairos offers ways in which the birds can help the gods. For example, if a man swore by Zeus *and* the Crow, and then broke his oath, the Crow would swoop down on him and peck out his right eye.

Drawing upon the same eloquent skills of rhetoric which he used originally to convince the birds of his plan, Pisthetairos persuades the three gods of his idea. Poseidon decides to cede the Sceptre of Divine Authority. At this point, Pisthetairos jumps in with: "The Birds are prepared to confirm Zeus' right to Hera, but in return they insist upon my having Basileia." After refusing to accept these new terms, Poseidon yields to the pressure of Herakles, who stands to gain nothing from Zeus' estate since he, Herakles, is a bastard.

So it is decided: Pisthetairos will marry Basileia. He knew that the gods were hungry, and his tactic to tempt them with food was successful, particularly with Herakles.

In the last section of the play, called the *exodos*, a messenger announces the arrival of Pisthetairos and Basileia. He is heralded as the "great Prince" of the birds, and, together, they are the King and Queen, splendid and beautiful, powerful and devoted. The birds form a circle around the couple and initiate a dance. Pisthetairos asks the birds to perform some odes in honor of his "triumph over the dangerous thunderbolts of Zeus."

When this is done, Pisthetairos invites his friends to follow the couple to the happy bed. As they drift off, a chorus chants: "O greatest of the gods: Hymen O! The wedding O!"

Commentary

The Birds is often considered to be the best example of Aristophanian comedy. It contains all the traditional elements and structures of his other plays, but it integrates them in a manner which makes the ultimate triumph more potent. It was this play which won second prize in the dramatic competition of 414 B.C. and which has been produced in numerous productions throughout the centuries, such as the modern Greek production directed by Karolos Koun.

The most helpful way to examine this play is to divide it into its component parts and focus on the major ideas of the playwright. First, a word on Aristophanes' dramatic structure might be of value.

The Old Comedy, of which *The Birds* is an example, was subdivided into a number of highly structured sections which the audience had grown to expect. The play began with relatively few characters, usually two or three, and in the initial scene, the audience was presented with the major idea or conflict of the play. At this point, the chorus appeared and sang its opening song; this was called the *parados.*

When the song was finished, the chorus moved to the area immediately in front of the spectators, down in the orchestra, and remained there for the duration of the play. Then the *agon* began, a contest wherein two rivals could compete for opposing principles (political, religious, etc.). One of the two was certain to win, and when this happened, the chorus would face the audience and sing its great song, the *parabasis.* This is the moment when the playwright was able to speak directly to his spectators, sparing no truth or harsh reality of the time.

In the case of *The Birds,* the play indeed begins with two characters, Euelpides and Pisthetairos. They present the major idea of the play – namely, their desire to establish a city where peace and happiness are possible. This section is sometimes called the *prologue.* The *parados* begins when the birds are summoned to hear the Athenian suggestion about CLOUDCUCKOOLAND. It lasts until Koryphaios, leader of the birds, is satisfied that the men mean no harm and that their ideas may be of interest to the birds.

This leads to the *agon,* where the two sides are represented by Pisthetairos/Euelpides and the birds. Pisthetairos is successful in persuading them of the benefits of his idea and this brings the contest to an end. The first *parabasis* then begins, covering the time when the chorus sings about the origins of the world and the creation of the birds. This is followed immediately by a series of 'scenes' which interchange with a second *parabasis* and several *chorikons,* short odes or choral interludes.

The comedy ends with a short *exodos* (i.e., final scene) in which the ritual of fertility is fulfilled. The critic Dudley Fitts says of this *exodos:* "The conclusion of the play is dictated not only by dramatic appropriateness – the marriage and deification of the Hero – but by ritual inheritance. Comedy culminates in marriage, and the final scene has overtones of an ancestral fertility rite. The chorus sings of the wedding of Zeus and Hera, thus equating Pisthetairos and Basileia with the King and Queen of Heaven. The ordinary man has found CLOUDCUCKOOLAND, his Utopia, and now becomes God. Like God, he insists upon the recital of his own meritorious exploits."

Enough of structure; these terms are useful only as boundaries and points of reference. What counts is your understanding of the play's ideologies and the reasons for which it is an excellent comedy. Herewith is a list of several points worth considering.

(1) **The Historical Background:** For the four decades prior to the production of *The Birds* (414 B.C.), Greece underwent changes which made the city-state the center of existence. Athens was the cultural hub of the civilization and, after the First Peloponnesian War (460-45 B.C.), the city experienced a high level of prosperity and confidence. It was a time of intense intellectual and artistic activity. But before long, war started up again in the form of the Great Peloponnesian War (431-04 B.C.). This destroyed many long-established traditions, particularly in the area of religion, and caused great numbers of refugees to enter the cities. A serious plague, combined with total defeat and the disaster at Syracuse, prompted the Greeks to lose faith in their gods.

This was the period during which *The Birds* was written. Aristophanes was disturbed with the political conflicts and enraged with his government's foolish conduct. The laws, courts, quacks of all sorts, and charlatans annoyed him. Though he sought to show both sides of the conflict, there is rarely any doubt in his plays about which viewpoint he represents. He resented foppish authority figures and their insistence on the value of war. At the same time, he criticized those individuals who pursued selfish intents at the expense of the group.

The idea of Athenian citizenship occupied him to some extent, and we have examples of this in *The Birds*. William Arrowsmith has said that "from the frequent allusions in the play to men who, technically ineligible, had somehow managed to get themselves enrolled as Athenian citizens, it is tempting to believe that proposals to revise the citizenship lists were in the air or had recently been carried out. The climax of these allusions comes in the final scene of the play, in which Pisthetairos attempts to prove that Herakles is technically a bastard (and hence cannot inherit Zeus' estate) because his mother was an ordinary mortal — that is, of 'foreign stock.'

This preoccupation with the item of citizenship is but one example of Aristophanes' revulsion for the governmental intrusions in private life. He believed that the individual was no longer free to choose his own lifestyle — that there was always someone ready to interrupt or rearrange or ruin one's plans. This is why Pisthetairos and Euelpides set out in search of the chosen land, their utopia — a dreamland which takes shape in the form of CLOUDCUCKOOLAND. They seek relief from the horrors of everyday Athenian life.

It was the sense of restlessness and unbounded ambition of the Athenians which had made the city great. But these very qualities, according to Aristophanes, could also destroy them. Arrowsmith adds: "[these qualities] also made Athens imperial and thereby propagated themselves; they were responsible for the senseless protraction of the Peloponnesian War and they would, Aristophanes believed, eventually destroy Athens as they had already destroyed the countryside of Attika and the virtue it fostered: the contented leisure of traditional order and the rural conservatism of peaceful life."

In short, the Athens of Aristophanes' time was a troubled, ambitious moment in Greek history. For the playwright, there were many infuriating injustices to expose.

(2) The Characters:

Euelpides: an old Athenian who is tired of the pettiness of Athens. With his companion, Pisthetairos, he is in search of a town where peace and happiness exist. But unlike Pisthetairos, he is neither brilliant nor persuasive and is shunted off early in the play to work on the construction of the wall. A flaw in Euelpides' character, insofar as becoming a bona fide resident of CLOUDCUCKOOLAND, is his obsession with material possessions — money, etc. He wants the happiness of a simple existence, yet he requires the amenities of a sophisticated society.

During the *agon* section of the play, Pisthetairos indicates that one of the ways to deal with uncooperative human beings is to send crows to peck out the eyes of their herds. Euelpides quickly retorts with: "Let me know in advance: I'll want to sell my yoke of oxen first." While neither the oxen nor the money from their sale would be of use in CLOUDCUCKOOLAND, Euelpides remains fixed to the values of his former society. Later in the same dialogue, he discovers that the birds would be helpful to humans by giving them tips on the weather: they could fly out to sea, check out the conditions, then return to the mainland with a weather report. Euelpides' response to that is, "I'll invest in a boat." Money has a stranglehold on him. As a consequence, he can never be free and serves no further purpose in the play. Aristophanes dismisses him promptly.

Pisthetairos: He is the savvy, profound member of the Athenian twosome who engineers the construction of CLOUDCUCKOO-LAND and assures the restoration of bird supremacy. He is weary of civilized life, mainly because it has become *un*civilized. In his eagerness to locate a serene existence, he draws upon his vast skills of rhetoric to convince the birds of his solid intentions. He evolves during the play from a beleaguered traveler to being the king of the new land. He is humorous, just, devoted to equitable law and order, and intolerant of quackeries. He is, to be sure, the very mouthpiece of Aristophanes.

Epops: Without Epops, we would have no drama. He is central to the action, and he uses his leverage to win favor for Pisthetairos. Epops is the Hoopoe bird. He was once a man, King of Thrace, who violated Philomela, sister of his wife Prokne. As punishment, the gods transformed him into a Hoopoe. He is considered by the birds to have wisdom and intelligence. So, when Pisthetairos arrives with his plan, Epops uses his influence to bring the birds to order. Thus, the former Tereus (which was his name as King of Thrace) becomes once again an important, respectable figure.

Koryphaios: This is the leader of the birds. At first, he is hostile and threatening toward Pisthetairos and Euelpides. But when he grasps some sense of what the Athenians have come to propose, his will softens and he becomes amenable to the idea. His role is crucial: he bears considerable influence on the bird community.

Prometheus: In mythology, Prometheus plays a colorful and often naughty role – or at least, from the gods' point of view. He ridiculed the gods and was punished by being chained to a rock on Mt. Caucasus, where a vulture preyed daily on his liver. He was rescued by Hercules, who killed the vulture. In this play, Prometheus displays his usual contempt for the gods by paying a quick trip to CLOUDCUCKOOLAND and warning the birds about Zeus' peace mission. It is thanks to Prometheus' advice that Pisthetairos is able to hold out for the brilliant and ingenious Basileia; this stroke of power gives Pisthetairos and his bride the firm stature of King and Queen, thereby reducing Zeus to the level of a eunuch.

Minor Characters: There is a host of important, though minor characters who parade through CLOUDCUCKOOLAND, one after another. They offer Aristophanes his chance to smack injustice into place, to retaliate against the charlatans of his time, and to voice protest against the policies of his government. Such is the case with the two poets (whose sugary verse cloys and annoys), the prophet (who sells bogus predictions), Meton (the surveyor who lays claim to land which is not his), the inspector and legislator (who, through some invisible authority, believe themselves privileged to exercise power over the birds), the parricide (who wants the benefits of the birds' rules without accepting responsibility), the informer (whose vicious occupation would make him the enemy of any peace-loving individual), and so on. There are countless others whom Aristophanes might have satirized, but for dramatic effect he has kept it to a tight minimum. Nonetheless, he takes swipes at representatives from the fields of religion, law, finance, and government. The point is clear: he has no use whatever for fakes, charlatans, quacks, and liars. Those who usurp fundamental human rights have no place in Aristophanes' utopia.

Iris: She is the daughter of Zeus, a messenger to the birds. Her purpose is purely functional: she represents the kingdom of the gods, which the citizens of CLOUDCUCKOOLAND intend to subjugate. That's all. She is a pretty young woman, but her charms count for nothing: Pisthetairos orders her out of his domain and uses particularly coarse language, which shows his absolute contempt for the gods. At the play's end, Basileia will symbolize the transition of power from the gods to the birds: she too is pretty and "manages Zeus, takes care of his thunderbolts and all the rest of his weapons – sagacity, legislation, rearmament, ideology, ultimatums, revenue officers, and jurymen." These are the people whom Aristophanes wishes to use as targets of satire. By marrying Basileia to Pisthetairos, he is able to effect this change.

(3) Health and Wealth: The idea of money is central to the comedy. Without money, man feels helpless and without influence. In the land of the birds, however, there is *no money*. When Euelpides discovers this, he adds immediately: "There go most of your problems." Euelpides symbolizes most human beings: he is obsessed with money and believes happiness is impossible without it. Money, for Euelpides, is indeed a problem.

But if we look at money as a mere symbol of buying power, we see that there are other ways of measuring influence and authority, of power and flexibility. The human sacrifices, under the new conditions of CLOUDCUCKOOLAND, will be offered to the birds, *not* to the gods. Therefore, birds will acquire power in their new position of leverage. Moreover, the gods – by virtue of losing their stronghold on human sacrifices – become subservient to the new masters, the birds. As one group loses its power, another obtains it. *Money* has not exchanged hands at all, yet *the principle of wealth* is nonetheless at stake.

There is an important message here for human beings. Obsession with money is a dangerous thing. Money is an elusive commodity, symbolic of power, but otherwise valueless by itself. When one thinks incessantly of money, one often, ironically, drives money away. Better to think of quality living, excellence in deed, achievement in action, and so on. Money is attracted magnetically to those who merit it. The constant groveling for it will serve little purpose. It is controlled by forces much greater than human will.

By freeing himself from a society governed by money, Pisthetairos achieves true purpose and happiness. He provides a quality service to the birds and obtains effective results through his actions. By the play's end, he is in a position of tremendous influence and power. And, if you will, he possesses considerable wealth. He is king, but he did not set out to accomplish this. His primary objective was to establish himself in an ambience of peace and tranquility. Through honesty and integrity, he attracted great fortune to himself. The laws of the universe have not changed since Aristophanes' time. The same results can be achieved by anyone truly motivated to improve his or her lot in life. It makes for a much healthier existence. When Koryphaios says to Pisthetairos: "But how will we give them health? That lies in the hands of the gods . . ." Pisthetairos responds: "Give them wealth, you give them health. They're really much the same."

(4) **Sexuality:** Aristophanes is no prude. He enjoys *language* and uses it to portray the most intimate of human behaviors. Among the latter is sexuality, which Aristophanes celebrates openly in all its nuances. There is no limitation or discrimination imposed randomly on the sexual act. Therefore, heterosexuality is regarded in the same open spirit as homosexuality – both of which are acknowledged as realities of the human experience.

Early in the play, in a dialogue with Epops, Pisthetairos says he would like to live in a place where men can feel and express their sexual reactions to other men. He mentions this, of course, to bring out the necessity for total obedience to one's innermost feelings. There would be no point in establishing a new city – CLOUDCUCKOOLAND – unless one got beyond the falsehoods of sophisticated civilization. "The Social Register," pokes Euelpides, "pains me in a spot I needn't describe." In other words, hypocrisy and pretense are highlighted as the cause of human deception – or at least are among the causes, if not effects.

A community devoid of such hypocrisy must surely acknowledge the need for honesty toward one's emotions. So without condemning homosexuality or endorsing it as the "way life should be," Aristophanes merely accepts the fact that homosexual feelings are part and parcel of every human experience. Freud, many centuries later, would confirm this in terms of psychoanalysis – despite the violent opposition from various social, religious, and political groups.

In *The Birds,* when Epops' wife, Prokne, the nightingale, comes out, Pisthetairos and Euelpides respond in sexual terms to her beauty:

> *Pisthetairos:* Almighty Zeus: Gosh, what a baby of a
> Birdie! What curves! What grace! What a looker!
> *Euelpides:* Gee! By god, I'd like to bounce between her
> thighs right now! . . . . I've got half a mind to kiss
> her.

So the same men who discussed affection for other men are the ones, here, who respond 'heterosexually' to Prokne. The problem seems not to be one of homo- versus heterosexuality, but rather one of terminology: *sexuality,* in *all* its manifestations, must be expressed openly or there is pent-up energy, frustration, and ultimately damage to the human being. This is not to say that the playwright recommends or encourages aggression whenever one feels like it. He is a proponent of moral restraint, within reason, but he believes that honesty should be the deciding factor in all human interactions. When we get beyond terminology and categorization, we are forced to realize that all human beings have a variety of sexual responses and capacities, and that little is gained by labeling individuals as homo, hetero, bisexual, and so on. The only purpose of such labeling is, perhaps, to alienate groups of people from society, thereby creating divisions within the human ranks. This is exactly what Aristophanes wishes to avoid in his new kingdom. To be sure, there are differences (e.g., man, birds, and gods), but the system is designed to allow maximum cooperation among the groups, a kind of mutual assistance.

When this attitude is applied to things sexual, it is usually met with opposition. But when human beings realize that they are composites of myriad and varying emotions, then perhaps unity can be restored to civilization. Is it too much to ask that people show support and concern for human beings whose lives differ from our own? We are all on earth for a purpose, but our purposes too are different from those of other people. Therefore, it is absurd to impose the same kinds of expectations on everyone. This is precisely why Euelpides and Pisthetairos have left Athens and why they are seeking a land where their goals may be accomplished, without outside interferences from selfish authorities. Peace and openness – those are the ideals of the playwright, in sexuality as well as in all other forms of human interaction.

(5) **Mankind and the Birds:** Aristophanes has fun with the notion that his birds are both literally and figuratively superior to mankind: their domain is in the sky, and they tower above their human counterparts. They are, quite clearly, *above* mankind. The two Athenians find society and contemporary life in Athens to their disliking. They are repelled by the injustice of laws, the meddling of the courts, the robbery of freedom by people who use their power unfairly, etc. There is pleasure for the men in the idea of cornering both humans and gods into an arena of helplessness. It would clear the way for liberty, self-assertion, and belief in equitable ideals. This says nothing, of course, about the possible resurgence of greed, hostilities, and ambition. But it opens the way for honest attempts at a superior lifestyle – one divorced from the nonsense which has become respectable in Athens.

Zeus and the gods represent the authorities of Aristophanes' time: government officials, religious figures, socially prominent individuals, and so on. They are the status quo of Greek society and play their roles astutely so as to remain in fashion, to maintain their positions of advantage. There is no justice or fair play in such an environment, and Aristophanes uses his minor characters to demonstrate the abuses of power: the legislator, the inspector, and the surveyor – all of them arrive to capitalize on the growing CLOUDCUCKOOLAND. None of them has any widespread concern for the new community; they are motivated by selfish desires and have nothing to contribute to the group. Even the two poets attempt to profit from their meager skills. By doing so, they embarrass themselves and belittle an otherwise beautiful art form.

The citizens of CLOUDCUCKOOLAND strive to restore dignity, honor, freedom, and honesty to their lives. They seek a return to their natural state – an existence unclouded with personal interest. They wish independence from undesirable authorities, and they hope only to establish for themselves a city designed to serve their needs. They are not revolutionaries anxious to overthrow and destroy; rather, they prefer to reassert themselves as worthy, respectable entities. No attempt is made to damage humans or deities. They only lay forth terms for freedom and cooperation. CLOUDCUCKOOLAND is not materialistic or terroristic in nature. It is a community conceived to unfetter – or unfeather? – its citizens from the bonds of servility.

THE CLOUDS (423 B.C.)

LIST OF CHARACTERS

Strepsiades

An Athenian father who is plagued by the daily, ever-increasing debts of his playboy son.

Phidippides

Strepsiades' son; he is fond of fast horses, fast chariots, and fast living. Reluctantly, Phidippides agrees to attend Socrates' school of logic and, after graduation, he uses Socrates' system of Unjust Logic to outwit his long-suffering father and cast him from the family home.

Socrates

Aristophanes offers us an inaccurate, satiric portrait of the master of Athens' renowned Think-tank, a school where well-heeled, monied young Athenians are taught to cleverly out-reason greedy creditors and muddle-headed, swaggering rhetoricians.

The Cloud Chorus

Basically, they function as Aristophanes' mouthpiece. They often address the audience directly, as well as comment on the goings-on onstage.

SUMMARIES AND COMMENTARIES

Summary

When the play begins, we see two houses onstage. One is small and dingy (this is Socrates' "Think-tank"), and next door is the spacious home of Strepsiades and his son, Phidippides. Phidippides is alternately snoring and talking in his sleep; in contrast, Strepsiades is unable to sleep. Suddenly, Strepsiades sits straight up in bed: his life has become a nightmare. He wonders aloud what he is going to do. The Peloponnesian War continues on, seeming as though it will never end, and now his son, Phidippides, is piling up debts on horses and horseracing that likewise seem as though *they* will never end. Strepsiades calls for a servant and begins to go through a pile of bills. He holds one up: Phidippides has bought yet another thoroughbred horse *and* another chariot. Horseracing – what absolute nonsense! Going in circles, faster and faster. God! That's what his debts have *him* doing – going ever faster in circles, trying to escape his creditors.

Phidippides groans and turns over; whatever *is* the matter with his father? The old man has tossed and turned and moaned all night long. Phidippides sighs and turns over and falls asleep immediately, dreaming once again of racing expensive new thoroughbreds. Strepsiades sighs; someday, with luck, he will die. Then Phidippides will inherit a vast fortune – of debts.

Strepsiades curses the matchmaker who first introduced him to Phidippides' mother. What a dumb country boy he was to be taken in by her perfumed, saffron-colored gowns and her city ways. Before he was married, he was such a happy bachelor – carefree, "rich in bees, in sheep, and olives"; he never bathed, and he never worried about anything. Then he married, and he began worrying – about everything. Yet, he can't fault his wife totally. She worked hard. While he was lounging about, drinking wine, she worked hard – that is, she worked hard spending everything he had.

When little Phidippides was born, Strepsiades had such great hopes for the boy. He remembers that he wanted to name the little baby "Pheidonides," meaning 'son of thrift.' His wife vetoed *that* suggestion. She wanted something more aristocratic, and she had her way; later, she spoiled the boy, filling his young imagination with a future full of flowing purple robes and fast racing chariots. Strepsiades tried to entertain his young son with tales of a time when they would be shepherds together, tending the goats and dressed in homemade fleecy, rough coats. Clearly, Phidippides became his mother's son.

And yet, Strepsiades says, there *may* be a way out; perhaps his insomnia was not in vain. Perhaps there does exist "a road to salvation." But he must be extremely careful to approach his son diplomatically, for he knows how stubborn, quick-tempered, and headstrong Phidippides can be.

Thus, he wakes Phidippides gently, as though his son were a tiny boy; sweetly, he asks Phidippides, his "little colt," if he loves his father, and, if so, to swear his love. Phidippides eagerly swears by "Poseidon, the god of horses," and Strepsiades is horrified: swear on *anything*, he pleads, but *not* on a horse. Horses have been the root of all his woes.

Phidippides asks what *is* the matter – what is at the bottom of his father's melodramatics, and Strepsiades explains that next door is the famous Think-tank, a place where men go and learn to reason by logic – "Unjust Logic," it is true, but logic nonetheless, and men use this logic to their advantage – especially to out-wit and out-reason their creditors. Strepsiades will pay for Phidippides' tuition if the boy will attend the school, learn their special kind of logic, and get rid of all of Strepsiades' creditors.

Phidippides is appalled. He knows the Think-tank well. He has seen the kind of people who attend that school; it is run by that ridiculous runt of a Socrates and attended by a bunch of pale-faced, puling ninnies. Why, if he agreed to attend school there, he'd be ashamed to look his favorite horse in the face. Besides, he'd lose his much-admired tan.

Strepsiades can take no more. No longer will he support Phidippides *or* his horses. He orders his son out of the house: "Go to the crows! Go hang yourself!" Nonplussed, Phidippides complies. Uncle Magacles will take him in; Uncle Magacles appreciates fast horses.

At his wit's end, Strepsiades decides to enroll at Socrates' Think-tank himself. He knows that he is an old man and that his memory isn't as good as it used to be, but *something* must be done. He is determined that he will at least *try* to learn Socrates' "Logic of Fine Distinctions and Subtleties." Courageously, he advances to the door of the Think-tank and knocks.

An arrogant student answers the door, sizes up Strepsiades, and berates him for knocking at the door "so stupidly." A good impression was *not* made; Socrates' classes are *not* easy; why, Strepsiades can't even knock right. But then, because Strepsiades looks so woebegone, the student beckons the old man forward. "We learn high mysteries here," he warns the old man. Socrates, the Master, can "seize fleas, measure their feet in wax, and calculate impossible distances."

Strepsiades is in awe: "Great Zeus! What a brain!" The student continues: it was Socrates who deduced, after much deep thought and logic, that gnats buzz through their *rears* and not through their noses, and "*that* took some doing."

Strepsiades is thunderstruck: "The arse of a gnat is a trumpet – what a splendid arsevation!" No wonder winning lawsuits is such a snap! "But there *are* hazards," the student warns. Only last night, Socrates was gazing open-mouthed at the moon, lost in thought, when a roof lizard relieved himself – in Socrates' open mouth. Naturally, a priceless thought was lost. Strepsiades nods gravely; he realizes the horror. He must enroll at once – before any more thoughts are lost. "Show me to Socrates. I want to be a student."

The Think-tank then opens up, and the audience sees Socrates' classroom, and high up in the air is Socrates himself, suspended in a basket. Beneath him are his disciples, looking half-starved and pale, anxiously examining the ground, looking more like specimens than like men. They certainly don't look like men of class, Strepsiades observes; they look more like the Spartan captives that Athens recently brought in. These are the intellectually "elite"? His bewilderment disappears, however, when the pupil explains that the reason why they are looking so intently *at* the ground is so that they can see "what is *below* the ground."

"Onions . . . truffles . . . why learning should be a snap," Strepsiades muses. He looks at them again and is puzzled as to why *all* of the students have their rears turned up toward heaven. The answer is obvious, says the student; while their minds are delving into the secrets of the earth, their rumps are divining the secrets of the stars, soaking up astronomy, as it were.

Strepsiades suddenly spots Socrates in his basket and asks who *that* is. *That* is the Master, he is told, and so Strepsiades hails him loudly: "Socrates! Sweet . . . [confusion overcomes the old man] Sweet Socratesicles!"

God-like, Socrates inquires if it is a "mere mortal" who addresses him. Naively, Strepsiades confesses that he simply wants to know what Socrates is *doing*. "I traverse air. I skip through the sky. I contemplate the Sun," Socrates answers, adding that only in this way can he "mingle the subtle essence" of his mind with Nature and the Things of Heaven. To remain forever on earth is to have one's mind eventually sapped into the soil. "That's what happens to watercress," he says.

This "revelation" of the mind's attracting the *sap* of watercress is overwhelming to Strepsiades. He is eager to learn more. Socrates descends in his basket, as Strepsiades zealously begs for more lessons, more wisdom. He tells Socrates that he has borrowed money, has amassed debts, that his creditors hound him night and day, and that only Socrates can solve his problems – by teaching him how to convince his creditors that he owes them absolutely nothing. Strepsiades has heard that Socrates is a "master of two kinds of reasoning," and the end result of one kind of logic results in "never repaying anything."

It's *that* logic that Strepsiades has come to learn, and he'll pay *anything* to learn it.

Socrates wants Strepsiades' word – and swearing by the gods is *not* good enough. Their value is too vacuous – *most* unreliable. Strepsiades looks uncomprehending. Thus, for the present, Socrates waves aside formalities: does Strepsiades truly wish intercourse with "yon Clouds and virgin Goddesses?" Strepsiades' answer is immediate and affirmative, so Socrates tells him to sit; soon Strepsiades will be "the flower of talkers." For the present, however, he must keep quiet. Socrates then majestically intones a prayer to the Air and the Ether and the Clouds.

There is a rumble of thunder, and under his breath, Strepsiades reproaches himself for not bringing a waterproof cap; if Olympos' clouds are summoned, no telling what kind of weather they'll bring with them.

A Chorus of Clouds hovers at the back of the stage, singing about their birth from the oceans' depths, their flight over lofty mountain heights, and their vast view of earth. They ask for yet a moment more before they come nearer so that they may rise even higher, thereby increasing their perspective and their knowledge. Socrates takes this opportunity to tell Strepsiades that he must not be afraid; he should feel free to address the Clouds and ask them for their wisdom.

But this is all too much for Strepsiades; he is in such fearful awe of Socrates *and* the Clouds that his bowels are upset. He pleads to find a bathroom – immediately. Socrates tells him to think positively; this sudden urge to defecate will pass. For the present, only "deep silence should be thine," he says, adding that the Cloud Chorus will momentarily break into song and reveal their "wisdom" – the secrets for foolproof "trickery, roguery, boasting, lies, and sagacity." Anxiously, Strepsiades looks heavenward, hoping to catch the first possible glimpse of these "omnipotent, celestial cobwebs."

The Clouds then silently assemble onstage, and Strepsiades pleads with them to speak, even though he is somewhat puzzled that they seem so human. Poets, he says, have always characterized the Clouds as being filled with dew and vapor, "waving their locks" and "swishing their impetuous tempests." Socrates tells the old man that the Clouds have assumed the form of women simply because they chanced to see the lovely Cleisthenes, the creator of choral singing; they could have been a herd of Centaurs, had they so desired.

When the Clouds begin to speak, these "Queens of Air" are *not* subtle. They ask what it is *now* that Socrates wants, noting that they perform "wonders" for him primarily because he is so full of "subtle nonsense," "hollow oration," and because he continuously goes about barefoot, as if he were a god. At these words, Strepsiades is overcome by such "august utterances," and Socrates assures him that the Clouds are the only true deities; "the rest are merely myths."

Strepsiades is shocked: "Is Zeus not a god?" Socrates assures him that "there is *no* Zeus." Strepsiades is dubious, and so Socrates "proves" that it is the Clouds – and not Zeus – who is responsible for the weather, thunder in particular. The teacher begins, lacing his specious arguments with such phrases as "Vortex of Air," "Necessity Sent," and "Compression Impelled," focusing finally on Strepsiades' bowels. Strepsiades' gas is air; the Clouds are air. Thunder is thunder, Socrates says, whether the thunder comes from the skies or from Strepsiades' bowels, and surely Strepsiades wouldn't dream of attributing his gas to *Zeus,* would he?

Strepsiades immediately feels better; he has always feared that rain, really, was Zeus urinating through a sieve. Cloud dew is ever so much better to consider. Similarly, then, Socrates "explains" that Zeus is not responsible for lightning either, and he convinces his new pupil to embrace his credo's Trinity: Space, Clouds, and The Eloquent Tongue. The Clouds agree to grant a special gift to Strepsiades: eloquence unparalleled.

Strepsiades shrieks: he doesn't want *eloquence;* he merely wants to be able to outwit his creditors. No trouble, says the Chorus, simply commit body and soul to the Sophists. The Clouds promise Strepsiades that very soon he will be besieged by crowds of debt-plagued men who will pay much money for his newly learned cunning. Socrates motions to Strepsiades, and the two men, turning in unison, enter the Think-tank.

The Cloud Chorus then speaks to the audience in a *parabasis.* They tell the audience that this particular comedy is Aristophanes' best – especially in its revised version. Originally, it won only Third Prize; now, it deserves a First Prize. The audience is further chided for not giving the Clouds themselves more credit. The Athenians, they say, are always planning some mad martial expedition – and would probably try to carry it out if the Clouds didn't intervene and send down rain and hailstorms. Moreover, the Athenians should give more thought and credit to the Moon, without whose phases all would be "naught but confusion."

Suddenly, Socrates bolts out of the Think-tank. He has *never* had a pupil "so inept, so stupid, and so forgetful!" He will try, however, one more time to teach Strepsiades metrics. He fails. Then Strepsiades fails to catch the nuances of rhythm; he can think of many things he would rather do with his finger than beat time to music. The gender of nouns escapes him completely. All he *really* wants to learn is How to Shirk Debts.

Socrates gives up and tells Strepsiades to be off: "Go feed the crows." In desperation, Strepsiades turns to the Clouds: what is he to do? They counsel him to try once more to convince his son to attend school at the Think-tank.

Surprisingly, Phidippides agrees to take lessons; after all, what else can he do for a mad father? "Tell the undertakers of his symptoms?" Understandably, Socrates is dubious about this new pupil; like father, like son. Nevertheless, he agrees to take him on, and so he brings out Right Logic and Wrong Logic for Phidippides' first lesson. Instead of lecturing their new pupil, however, the two men set to arguing, and the Cloud Chorus finally has to separate them. Right Logic yearns for the good old days when sons respected their elders and didn't loiter all day at the public baths.

Wrong Logic is incensed; he says that Right Logic would make sissies of Athens' best young men. Not so, says Right Logic. He would exercise health into their blood; he says that Wrong Logic would exercise one thing only: erections. In contrast, he would dwell on erect *posture* – broad shoulders, full chests, bright eyes, and tight biceps, and all his pupils' thoughts would be *above* the waist.

The Cloud Chorus beams; sweet indeed are the Ancient Virtues. Wrong Logic snarls: he'll win this argument yet! He challenges Right Logic to name *one man* who has gained anything by being chaste. He says that Life should be filled with women, feasting, and drinking. Then, if one *is* caught in adultery, which most men do commit at one time or another, the "worldly" man can at least defend himself. Above all, one must have a good defense – for if a man cannot defend himself, hot coals are rammed up his rear. If a man can prove that Zeus is *the* prime example of an Adulterer Unparalleled, however, then he can avoid the hot coals. Imagine a mamma's boy, tutored by Right Logic, and then caught in adultery; he would be lost – absolutely lost.

Right Logic is forced to agree; given the weaknesses of human nature and its wont to "sport between the sheets," a man *ought* to know how to rationalize his nocturnal games. Thus, Wrong Logic triumphs, and he exits with his new pupil, Phidippides.

In a second *parabasis,* the Clouds warn the audience that if they know what's good for them, they'll give this play the award for first place. Otherwise: unending drought, and then tile-tearing torrents!

Several days pass, and Strepsiades appears with a present for Socrates. His son has learned well. He has become a true Sophist: "keen and polished of tongue is he." Pasias, a moneylender, enters and, later, Amynias, another moneylender, enters and Strepsiades, proud of his son's new verbal gymnastics, tries some of his own. He merely appears crazy, however, and the two moneylenders exit, more furious than before.

The Cloud Chorus bemoans old Strepsiades' attempts to mimic his son's fraudulent reasoning. They predict bad things, and no sooner have they finished than Strepsiades is driven onstage, out of his own house, by Phidippides. Using Wrong Logic's reasoning, he "proves" that he should be allowed to strike his father "justly" because Strepsiades has reverted to his second childhood, and children deserve punishment. Strepsiades asks for mercy from the Clouds, but they refuse to help him: he should have paid his debts instead of trying to cheat his creditors. Phidippides says that his father is as nutty as a fruitcake.

Nutty? Crazy? Strepsiades will show them what he is capable of. He seizes a blazing torch and sets fire to Socrates' Think-tank. It bursts into flame, and Strepsiades purrs to one of the confused, incoherent pupils, "Why, I'm only *subtly* arguing with the beams of the Think-tank." Socrates appears on the burning roof, and Strepsiades hails him: "How wonderful it is to contemplate the sun!"

Blasphemy has been banished at last, and the Cloud Chorus leaves the stage, its leader remarking, "You know, I think we played our parts rather well today, don't you?"

Commentary

This version of *The Clouds* is clearly not the version which was defeated by Cratinus' *Wine Flask* during one of the Comedy Competitions of the Great Dionysia celebrations. In this version of *The Clouds,* the Chorus complains crankily about Aristophanes' originally winning only Third Prize. Almost all critics today, however, agree that this version of *The Clouds* is probably basically unchanged from the earlier version; perhaps it is more polished, its wit more biting, and its broad farce more sexual, but it is basically the play that was awarded Third Prize. Yet it is considered one of Aristophanes' best comedies. One should remember this fact, as well as the fact that the play has a glaring dramatic flaw. Aristophanes wanted to satirize the Sophists, popularizers of a new philosophy that denied the possibility of man's *ever* reaching objective truth. For the most part, these Sophists were not native Athenians; they came from such diverse places as Chalcedon in Bithynia, from Thrace, from Samos, Sicily, and other foreign city-states and countries, and they came to Athens because Athens was renowned as the intellectual center of the Hellenic world. Aristophanes did not like new, foreign philosophies replacing the tried-and-true wisdom of ancient Greece. In addition, he did not like these new Sophists taking only the richest young men for pupils and promising them *not* objective truth after they were "graduated," but, instead, "worldly wisdom." Aristophanes was extremely conservative; he was very pro-Athens, and he feared that the young men of his time were becoming esthetes, fencers of fancy rhetoric, instead of stolid, manly warriors. When Aristophanes was writing his comedies, Athens was fighting for its very life, after more than twenty years of continual defeats by Sparta, and satire was the weapon that Aristophanes chose to point out to his fellow Athenians the emptiness and the destructiveness of the "new thinking" of the Sophists.

But, in order to pungently satirize these Sophists, Aristophanes needed a "character," someone whom the audience would recognize on sight and laugh at before the character had uttered even a single line. He needed a human sight gag as a hook for his comedy, and so he chose an almost legendary "character" of Athens: Socrates. Twenty-four years later, Socrates would be condemned to death — 399 B.C.—for "corrupting the youth of Athens"; concerning his accusers at that time, he would say, "I cannot tell you the exact names of my accusers — except in the case of a 'comic' poet"; he was referring, of course, to Aristophanes.

Thus, everyone with some degree of learning knew about Socrates. Physically, the old philosopher was grotesque. He was short, fat, and snub-nosed; his eyes bulged unnaturally, his nostrils were enormous, and his mouth was generous to a fault. In short, Socrates looked like a burnt-out old satyr. And although Socrates never had what could be called a "school of philosophy," he did have a large following of young men who were fascinated by his courage to dare to question everything and anything. These young Athenians were rebels, and Socrates was their leader.

But if there was anything that Socrates was *not,* he was definitely *not* a Sophist. As we said, he never organized any literal "school of philosophy," and he never accepted money for his teachings. He talked freely to anyone who would listen and/or talk to him, and he would talk to anyone who would try and answer his multitude of questions. He loved intellectual inquiry for its own sake. In theory, Socrates believed that after one repeatedly realized the inadequacy of one answer after another, this person would realize how little he truly knew; thus, he could begin anew, searching for truth and wisdom – without prejudice and stock answers – and hopefully, arrive at a sound answer. Indeed, one of Socrates' claims to fame was that he "knew nothing." He loudly disavowed being omniscient and all-knowing. He was dedicated solely to inquiry. He rejected absolutely the so-called "new thinking" of his time. Thus, Aristophanes did *not* make a good choice for the pivotal caricature/character of his comedy. Socrates was, literally, a comic *looking* fellow, but most theatergoers of the time knew that he was *not* a Sophist. He was, if anything, staunchly *anti-*Sophist.

Today's audiences, in contrast, are not as familiar with Socrates as were the audiences in Aristophanes' time. Therefore, for today's audiences, *The Clouds* is infinitely more accessible as a piece of comedy. They can easily equate Socrates with the popular, modern caricature of the addle-brained, absent-minded professor. Also, modern audiences can identify instantly with the desperate frustration of a father whose son's reckless spending brings them ever nearer to the Poor House. Strepsiades is unlearned; if he can convince his son to attain, as it were, a "college education," all their troubles will be over. All their debts will be paid by *not* being paid – and all because Phidippides will have learned to outwit the many creditors who are hounding Strepsiades.

In a strictly high-brow, literary sense, then, *The Clouds* can be said to fail because of Aristophanes' critical flaw in construction. But, for audiences today, *The Clouds* is good comedy. We laugh at the man of excess, and both Socrates and Strepsiades are men of excess, men outside the norm. Strepsiades has excessive debts; he is a loser, his wife sounds like a shrew, and his son is a wastrel. All these are the trappings of excess. Socrates is excessively full of pompous, empty, fraudulent theories. And in the end, both men are "punished" for their excesses. No one will help Strepsiades after he is turned out of his house by a son whom he "educated" for one purpose only – to avoid paying debts.

Likewise, Socrates is punished. His devious Think-tank is burnt by the hopelessly frustrated Strepsiades. We must remember that Aristophanes was a conservative. He wanted Athens to embrace the Old Virtues; he believed that a society was best if it accepted *traditional* wisdom and "the order of things." He rejected the liberal social reforms that his fellow playwright Euripides encouraged. These liberals, these "progressives," were suspect. Curiously, the genre of comedy has continued to flourish by often using a "liberal," or a deviant, or a "crackpot" as the butt of a two-hour joke. This observation applies as well to the comedy in comic strips. It is Charlie Brown's frailties and his failures that we laugh at; Charlie Brown doesn't and can't meet the "norms" of society. He is an Outsider. He is a loser. Lucy, in contrast, is Authority and Conservative Reliability. She is reliable to excess – and that makes her also a comic character, but she is, above all, the Norm. And it was the Old Standards, Old Values, and Old Traditions that Aristophanes was yearning for when he conceived *The Clouds*. He hoped to expose the folly of faddish, foolish empty thinking. He wanted to attack "modern" education and make people realize, through laughter, how ridiculous it all was. Thus, he ridicules Socrates and his pupils, and at the end of the comedy, the Think-tank is burned to the ground, and, symbolically, "modern education" has been eradicated.

For Aristophanes, the theater was a forum and a pulpit. He used it to preach from, but he chose to deliver his sermons in comedies rather than in tragedies. Tragedies revealed Truth by the catharsis of suffering. Comedies revealed Truth by the catharsis of releasing laughter. Because of Aristophanes' genius, comedies were not merely light exercises in wit. His comedies are serious business. Underneath the abundance of X-rated puns and scatological jokes is the spirit of a reformer who spent most of his adult years trying to eke out a living during the long Peloponnesian War. Not surprisingly, Aristophanes came to realize that war was probably man's most expensive and futile exercise. He loathed war, and he wrote a rather large number of anti-war comedies, all bitterly mocking strife and exposing the criminality of war.

Thus, in comparison with Aristophanes' satiric attacks on war, *The Clouds* is almost gentle, focusing on thought and verbal battles rather than on strife and physical combat. Yet, even in this play, Aristophanes rails against war. When the play opens, even before Strepsiades bemoans his mounting debts, he curses the long years of the Peloponnesian War. Besides disrupting the state's business of civilizing and governing its citizens, the War has recently caused new laws to be enacted: now, farming has been forbidden, and slaves can no longer be punished by sending them off to do backbreaking farm labor. A person must therefore be careful how he punishes his slaves; otherwise, they might defect to the enemy. This is yet one more plague on Strepsiades – he can't even take out his frustrations on his slaves. Of course, if Strepsiades had not been henpecked and if he had been "man enough" to rear his son as *he* wanted to – leading a productive, raw country life, driving in the goats at night – Phidippides would never have been allowed to amass all his debts. But Strepsiades failed, and so we have, as a result, one of the central figures of this comedy – a character who never appears onstage: Strepsiades' *wife:* a blue-blooded, stuck-up bitch, a sure-fire caricature even today. She molded the good-for-nothing son who will, at the end of the play, use Sophist logic to banish Strepsiades from his own home.

Ironically, Aristophanes' description of Strepsiades' wife sounds very much like Socrates' shrew of a wife: Xantippe. If legend is correct, Xantippe was a loud-mouthed, viciously nagging fishwife if ever there was one – impossible to live with. More than one critic has suggested that it was her nagging which drove Socrates out of the house and into the streets, where he began teaching his unique way of attaining wisdom – through inquiry. And of course, since Socrates never charged any money for his teaching, Xantippe reproached him nightly for their poverty and for their accumulating debts. In *The Clouds,* Strepsiades' wife has spent all the money he has, his son has also turned into a spendthrift, and there is no one whom Strepsiades can take out his frustrations on. He can't beat his slaves, and he can't bring himself to beat his son. But he finally does kick his son out of the house, an act which leaves him absolutely all alone, lost in a sea of hungry creditors.

Thus, Aristophanes sets up "the rustic," an old man who is both ignorant and illiterate, vs. a haughty, pseudo-learned "intellectual" – two favorite targets for satirists. The comedy is played broadly by the rustic, and archly by the pedant; and to the delight of the Athenians, Aristophanes liberally peppers his comedy with "bathroom humor."

One should not be offended by this; remember that the genre of comedy was originally derived from lusty masquerades and mime, involving raucous singing and carousing by revelers wearing grotesque masks and enormous, strapped-on phalluses, all in a wild celebration of fertility. We should not be overly surprised, therefore, to discover how Aristophanes chooses to characterize the Sophists and their "new learning"–that is, when Strepsiades himself desperately tries to learn the Sophists' "new truths," we learn that Socrates has discovered that a gnat buzzes through its anus–and not through its nose; here, we have a graphic indication of what Aristophanes thought of the "new learning." As for the chief guru of the Sophists, Socrates himself, we learn that recently he "lost" a priceless insight into the Nature of Things when a nocturnal lizard accidentally defecated into Socrates' open mouth as he was gazing at the moon.

In addition, these young Sophists study not only with their minds gazing earthward, but also with their posteriors upended, their anus-eyes directed toward the heavens. Clearly then, from the very beginning of this comedy, Aristophanes' satire was directed toward what he believed to be the deterioriating culture of his times. *The Clouds* is stinging. Aristophanes believed that Athens' morals were degenerating, debts were bankrupting the city-state, and, meanwhile, the city's leading thinkers, (embodied in the character of Socrates) were suspending themselves, like Socrates, above critical, earthly concerns.

But it is, ironically, the Clouds themselves who provide us with some of the best comedy in the play, and not the individual comic characters. The Clouds are a sassy bunch, imperial in their posturings, and defiant of everyone. They boast of their immortal nature and of their ability to "sweep the whole world with a look."

Like Socrates, they believe that they contain "all wisdom." They can, if they wish, water the earth with delicious rain, or they can, on a whim, slash the soil with a flood of hailstones and tornadoes. Or they can raze the world with years of drought. They state forthrightly that they protect Socrates because he's such an air-head, "just another windbag." Additionally, they speak for Aristophanes, stating unreservedly that this particular comedy is the best of all the comedies that Aristophanes has written: *this* comedy doesn't rely on phallic jokes or indecent sexual snickerings, and it does *not* poke unnecessary fun at "bald-heads." (Aristophanes had suffered a shockingly fast loss of hair, and he was extremely self-conscious about being bald; he deeply resented other writers of comedies who made bald-headed men into comic dolts and dummies.) *The Clouds,* says the Cloud Chorus, relies on nothing but *its own merits.* This bit of over-reacting defensiveness is nonsense. If Aristophanes was being serious, he unintentionally enriched his comedy immeasurably. By putting these words into the mouth of the collective Chorus, he reminded the audience of the plethora of phallic humor, as well as the satiric portrait of the doddering (and probably balding) old Strepsiades, and Socrates as well. The Clouds, therefore, are revealed to be as full of hot air as the caricature of Socrates is, and it is these very Clouds which Socrates worships and from whom he receives his "wisdom." These indeed are the new "gods and goddesses" of the "new learning," those who have replaced the old conservative values and the "conventional" gods of Athens.

The Clouds is superb comedy – if one can forgive Aristophanes for using the noble Socrates as the butt of this satire. To expose fraud onstage is always a sure-fire source of comedy, and Aristophanes does just that, using fantasy, rustics, ribaldry, spicy dialogue – all to expose what he believed to be The Great Lie of Sophism. Civil and cultural corruption *could* be saved, he believed, and instead of showing its downfall in a tragedy, he exposed its ridiculous aspects, and let people laugh instead of lament. In both cases, drama provided release from frustration and suppression – sexual and social – and Aristophanes chose to try and remedy the ills of his beloved Athens through laughter and satire. His comic mockery is often savage, but it is always on-target. And it speaks well of Athens' progressive, enlightened democracy that the city fathers would allow such irreverence. The dramatic license that Aristophanes enjoyed is rare – especially in a nation that is at war. Part of the so-called glory-that-was-Greece lies in this very phenomenon of the comic tradition. Such catharsis was new to the Western world, and it has survived – despite despots and dictatorships. The value that a civilization places on laughter is often a measure of its greatness and of its psychologically sound serenity and stability. Luckily, Greece was wise enough to recognize that laughter was healthy and healing, and it was lucky enough to have a genius like Aristophanes who could translate that attitude into lasting masterpieces. Comedy was recognized as a genre, along with tragedy, and drama was brought to earth – all in the name of fun and fantasy. Aristophanes was a breath of fresh air, a release and a contrast to the abundant, dark Greek tragedies; his plays were healthy, corrective counterparts to his peers' ritualized recreations of death as a necessary ingredient for knowledge and rebirth. Aristophanes' brilliance and genius are revealed not only by the comedies, but also by his continued experimentation and refinement of the new genre. In *The Clouds*, we have a timeless model of wit, daring to challenge new notions – not by didacticism or edict, but by wit and rebellion, using the absurd to enlighten. *The Clouds* is both tawdry and sublime – a comic touchstone. To contemplate it is, in the words of both Socrates and Strepsiades, "to contemplate the sun."

THE FROGS (405 B.C.)

LIST OF CHARACTERS

Xanthias

The slave of Dionysos; he has a remarkable sense of humor and endures his master's many moods with an enlightened sort of irony.

Dionysos

The god of theater who decides to bring back his favorite playwright from the Underworld. He is a coward and amusingly ferocious with his servant Xanthias.

Herakles

He is an authority figure who has been to the Underworld; he argues with Dionysos that there are many better playwrights than Euripides. He insists that Dionysos is crazy to go to Hell, but Dionysos goes anyway, wearing Herakles' uniform.

Aiakos

The doorman at Pluto's dwelling.

Charon

The ferryman of Hades. He announces the various destinations to which he will navigate passengers.

Plathane

A young waitress.

Aeschylus

A playwright from Athens. He wrote ninety tragedies and received public prizes for forty of them. He was killed when a tortoise fell from the beak of an eagle and struck him on the head, a most fitting death for a tragedian.

Euripides

A writer of tragedies, born at Salamis. He studied ethics under Socrates and wrote his tragedies in a lonely cave. He is the alleged author of twenty-five tragedies, of which nineteen remain. He died in the savage mouths of dogs, whose teeth ripped him to shreds.

Pluto

The son of Saturn and Ops; he inherited his father's kingdom, along with his brothers Jupiter and Neptune. Pluto's share is the Underworld. It was he who grabbed Proserpina as she gathered flowers in the fields; he abducted her, married her, and made her queen of Hell.

SUMMARIES AND COMMENTARIES

Summary

The play begins with a Prologue outside the house of Herakles in Athens (you will oftentimes see it spelled Heracles). Dionysos, god of fertility and wine, and patron of drama, and his slave Xanthias are on stage, equipped for an excursion, with Xanthias bent double under the luggage, and Dionysos on foot. Xanthias complains about the excessive load, but Dionysos reminds him that it is the *donkey* who carries the load, *not* Xanthias.

Having arrived at Herakles' front door, they knock and are let in. Herakles laughs at Dionysos' appearance: he is at once heroic and effeminate, wearing a lion skin draped over a saffron gown, plus bedroom slippers and carrying a large, knotty club. Dionysos and Herakles exchange quips about a desire which overwhelmed Dionysos while reading Euripides' play *Andromeda*: Herakles wonders whether Dionysos felt a desire for a woman, a young boy, a grown man, etc., but none of these is correct.

Dionysos confesses that he has a longing for the poet-playwright *Euripides,* even though he is dead, but Dionysos intends to find him: "No merely human force shall hinder me from seeking him out." He has decided to venture into the Underworld to locate the deceased playwright, for he worries about the state of theater, now that the great Euripides is gone. Dionysos hopes to bring him back from the dead.

Herakles mentions a number of contemporary dramatists, but Dionysos is undaunted: none of the latter can hold a candle to Euripides. They are all minor tragic poets: "I don't care where you look, you won't find a poet today who is really generative." (Note: by 'poet,' Dionysos means 'dramatist.') To prove his point, Dionysos quotes several verses from one of Euripides' plays, claiming that *no one* can create as beautifully as the dead writer.

Herakles cannot believe what he hears: "It's trash and you know it," he tells Dionysos. But the latter avows his devotion to Euripides, and he announces to Herakles that he is on his way to Hell in the latter's uniform and seeks information from him; he wishes to know what Hell was like when Herakles was there: "The sights? The shops? Whorehouses, taverns, restaurants, the hotels with the fewest bedbugs?"

Herakles tells him the quickest way to get there. It is not a pleasant trip since he will pass across a dismal lake (via a ferryboat manned by Charon), onto a land covered with snakes and disgusting beasts, through a mighty swamp with an almighty stench ("Here they throw criminals – men who cheat their young male prostitutes of pay for the pleasure they've given"). There, he will also see the Initiates – those happy crowds of men and women who are participants in the Eleusinian Mysteries, celebrated annually in honor of Persephone and Demeter, goddesses of fertility.

Herakles bids him farewell just as four undertaker's assistants arrive with a corpse. Dionysos asks the Dead Man to carry his luggage to Hell for him; when the Dead Man begins to negotiate a price for his services, Dionysos says that the price is too expensive. Huffily, the Dead Man orders the undertaker's aids to carry him off. This ends the Prologue.

Scene I shifts to the shores of the Infernal Lake. Charon awaits them in a dilapidated skiff. When they greet Charon, he treats them formally: "Who are you, coming from the world of woe and care?" Dionysos identifies himself simply as "Me." He then gets on board with Charon; Xanthias, however, must walk around the lake since he is a slave. Charon orders Dionysos to row; but the latter cannot conceive of this: "Me? Row? Unshipbroken, unoceanized, unoared? How can I row?" Charon replies that it is easy: Dionysos will be accompanied by a musical chorus of frogs who will sing: "Brekekekex koax koax, we are the swamp-children, greeny and tiny, fluting our voices as all in time we sing our koax koax koax koax koax."

Dionysos is annoyed with the rowing, and he shouts out at the frogs: "My arse is sore, koax koax. . . my hands are ablaze, my bottom's a wreck! In a minute or two you'll hear it speak." When they serenade him further, he protests with: "Silence, you lily-pad lyrists, koax!" The more he complains, however, the more loudly they sing. When all reasoning fails, he breaks wind loudly, and they suddenly become silent. The boat reaches the other shore.

As Scene II begins, the men have landed on the shores of Hell. Xanthias arrives on foot and welcomes his master to the Underworld. He then suggests to Dionysos that they vacate the premises, recalling the words of Herakles: Hell is a dangerous place to be.

Dionysos feigns a macho quality and scorns his slave for being cowardly. The latter decides to get even with Dionysos by pretending to see the Empusa, a horrible monster. This causes Dionysos to jump back and forth to avoid being harmed. His point proven, Xanthias announces that the goblin has vanished.

Dionysos asks his servant to swear three times that the Empusa is gone, and Xanthias notices the fear-inspired, soiled plops in his master's pants:

> *Dionysos:* I went all white when I saw the Empusa [a goblin
> noted for its incessant changes of form].
> *Xanthias:* Yes; and part of your robe went all brown.

When the Initiates begin to sing, as Herakles predicted they would, Dionysos and Xanthias lie low and listen. With torches flaring, the Initiates enter, and the *parados* begins. They are dressed for their annual procession to the earthly Eleusis (see Commentary for explanation). It is in this section that Aristophanes addresses the audience directly, via the Chorus.

Koryphaios, leader of the Initiates, announces that all evil-doers must leave, and the Chorus then praises the goddess Athena (after whom Athens was named) and sings a hymn to Demeter, queen of the fields. Demeter is summoned to be Mistress of Ceremonies for their barbed, satiric plays. Koryphaios then pays tribute to Dionysos:

> Sing the adorable god who leads us all in our dancing; sing
> Dionysos the fair, draw him to us in song.

With this, the Chorus launches into an attack on three Athenians: Archedemos (for being unable to prove his citizenship), Cleisthenes (for being "pederast, pig, and effeminate"), and Callias (for having sex with too many women – "the girls look once, and then give in"). When Dionysos ventures out of his hiding spot to ask for directions, Koryphaios gladly sends him to Pluto's residence, "that austere dwelling."

Dionysos opens Scene III with a particularly awesome, thought-provoking, and beautiful line: "How does one knock at the door of Hell?" He is disguised as Herakles. In a parody of Euripides' inflated style, the doorman Aiakos curses at Herakles/Dionysos, the "wretched, rash, intruding, hateful cheat." Dionysos, in shock, defecates again. Since Xanthias claims to be bold, Dionysos quickly switches identities with him by exchanging Herakles' lion skin.

In Scene IV, Persephone's maid lets them in and gushingly tempts Herakles/Xanthias with some "lovely girls, all perfumed and plucked, not one of them over fifteen." Dionysos, infuriated, orders that he and his servant swap costumes again. The idea of Xanthias in bed with a young nymphet causes him no small amount of envy.

Plathane, a young waitress, spots Herakles/Dionysos and identifies him as a man who was guilty of gluttony in the past. She conspires with an elderly, saggy-breasted barmaid to do him in: they intend to throw him in court that very day.

Dionysos, frightened for his life, exchanges the Herakles costume again with Xanthias. Then Aiakos appears, carrying a horsewhip, and he tells three constables to arrest Herakles/Xanthias for dog theft. Xanthias disavows any responsibility for crime and orders the men to torture his 'slave' (i.e., Dionysos): "Hang him by the thumbs, or stretch him on the ladder, or flay him, or pour vinegar up his nose." Dionysos argues that he *cannot* be tortured: "I am a god."

Aiakos tells Xanthias and Dionysos to strip; he then proceeds to lash their buttocks: whichever one yells "Uncle" first is *not* the god. The lashes continue as the two men try not to show discomfort; in their mounting agony, surprisingly, they respond to the pain by quoting verses from Sophocles and other playwrights. Aiakos decides to ask the King and Persephone which one is a god. Xanthias responds, "A good idea, but I wish you'd thought of it sooner."

In the *parabasis*, Aristophanes speaks once again to the audience through the Chorus. This interlude from the play focuses on the deteriorating situation of the war which threatens Athens. Retaliations and political recriminations abound, and he pleads for tolerance even though disaster looms on the horizon. He is concerned here, as in other plays, with the rights of aliens – people who are thrown out of Athens when unable to prove their citizenship.

Scene V opens with a conversation between one of Pluto's serv-ants and Xanthias. Pluto's servant clearly admires Xanthias; they share a common function in life. They hear a noise from within: a dispute between Aeschylus and Euripides. It is a tradition in Hades that when a great artist dies, he sits next to Pluto at the Prytaneion – which is what happened when Aeschylus arrived. But when an even greater talented man arrives, the current "master" has to yield up his place. The dispute between Euripides and Aeschylus stems from their disagreement over which one is greater.

The factions for each dramatist have insisted on a poetry contest "to determine which artist really deserves the Chair." Almost no one supports Aeschylus since, according to Pluto's servant, "Respectable men are few in this place." So Pluto decides to hold a contest and let a judgment be made. What's more, it is decided to name Dionysos as the judge ("He *does* know his poetry, after all.").

Scene VI is a discussion between Aeschylus, Dionysos, and Euripides. Euripides argues that he is better than Aeschylus, but the latter vows to expose "how this Master of the Limp[-wrist] has fooled all Athens with his cast of 'cripples.'"

Aeschylus and Euripides sit on stools opposite each other in preparation for the contest. Dionysos announces the rules: "Let's not waste time, gentlemen. What we want is elegance: no pointless decora-tion, no second-hand imagery." Euripides then launches into an attack on Aeschylus' dramatic structure; he argues that his own plays con-tain real-life situations – not pomp and pretense, as in Aeschylus' dramas.

What ensues is a detailed volleying of criticisms and defenses of their individual work. (The essential points are summarized in the Commentary.) When Euripides presents his arguments, Dionysos sides with *him;* but when Aeschylus counters the attack, Dionysos changes corners and takes *the older poet's* defense. To resolve the dispute, they weigh Aeschylus' verses against Euripides' in a large cheese-scale. Aeschylus wins three rounds of competitions, to the dismay of Euripides.

Pluto arrives, crowned and sceptered. When Dionysos complains about having to choose between two such capable dramatists, Pluto in-structs him to make his choice and take the winner back to earth with him. So Dionysos chooses Aeschylus. Euripides is bitter about being abandoned to the dead, but Dionysos replies with one of Euripides' own verses: "Which of us can say that life's not death's twin brother?"

Pluto bids them farewell as Aeschylus grants his Chair to Sophocles, "second among the serious poets." The Chorus ushers Aeschylus on his way to earth: "May he heal the sick State, fight the ignoble, cowardly, inward foe and bring us peace."

Commentary

This is one of Aristophanes' less well-known plays and, some argue, less important. It is essentially a study in literary criticism designed to expose the major shortcomings of Euripides' plays. Structurally, it is not a sound drama: the playwright veers from subplot to subplot (for example, whatever happened to the attempt of Plathane to send Dionysos to court?) in a way which suggests Aristophanes' need to cover several 'topics' within one comedy. So while it is important that Aristophanes finally achieves his goal of demystifying Euripides, he arrives at this effect only by way of a visit to Herakles, a boat-ride through Hell, and so on. The play's title derives, strangely, from a subordinate chorus of frogs which appears in only one scene. One might surmise that Aristophanes wished to compare the writing of Euripides to the Brekekekex, koax, koax of the frogs.

The critic Louis E. Lord has stated that "the contest between Euripides and Aeschylus in *The Frogs* is one of the very earliest and one of the best documents in the whole history of literary criticism." Aristophanes possessed, as the critic Saintsbury says: ". . . both generally and in this particular instance, all the requisites for playing the part of literary critic to perfection, with one single exception – the possession, namely, of that wide comparative knowledge of other literatures which the Greeks lacked." The whole critique of both poets is equally keen and, allowing for strong personal prejudice, surprisingly fair. To have produced such apt parodies of styles so different, to have noted with such unerring insight the weakness and the power of each author [for Euripides' defense is not weak], to have been concrete and vivid where Aristotle is only general and vague – in short, to have produced the first great and influential document in literary criticism constitutes one of Aristophanes' claims to immortality.

Not only was this play among the first examples of literary criticism, but it also provided important suggestions to the government of Athens concerning the alien problem. Aristophanes advocates the enfranchising of the exiles and, partly because of his message in *The Frogs,* he convinced the State to do this. Political and social commentaries are woven into the fabric of the play through devices such as the Chorus, the *parados,* etc. *The Frogs* was produced at the Lenaian Festival of 405 B.C. during the twenty-sixth year of the Peloponnesian War, shortly before the final defeat of Athens at the hands of Sparta. Any intelligent comments made during this critical period were likely to have been considered by the officials in power.

The play is vital for reasons other than its literary criticism. Aristophanes takes an interest in the philosophical questions of his time, so that Dionysos, on a mission which portends strictly dramatic interactions, becomes involved in the quest for restoring important values to the civilization of Athens. The critic Dudley Fitts has said in an introduction to his amusing translation of this play: "At the beginning of this play Dionysos goes in quest of Euripides because he is a fashionable, decadent, 'modernist' dramatist. There is no question of serious purpose. But in the end he decides that Aeschylus, not Euripides, must be returned to Athens, because the salvation of the state depends upon restoring the manly conservative principles for which the elder poet stands. What has happened is not unusual in comic satire: the initial raillery has become serious."

The Dionysos/Xanthias relationship is humorous and energetic. The characters complement one another in a fashion not unlike that of Don Quixote/Sancho Panza: they are opposites and represent quite different values. Dionysos, for all his godliness, is a coward. He is forever soiling his pants and hiding behind nearby trees. Xanthias, however, is a good soul, devoted to the tedious item of serving a nincompoop, even when tempted by the more bawdy side of his nature to create havoc or confusion.

When Dionysos utters his comment about being a god ("I am a god"), Aristophanes highlights the privileged status, the authority and sense of indestructibility which attend such "confessions." The sentence is a sudden stroke of arrogance. The "god" is shown to be as vulnerable as the human being.

Two points worth mentioning:

(1) **The Initiates' procession to the earthly Eleusis:** Eleusinia was the great festival observed by the Athenians every five years at Eleusis in Attica. It was the most celebrated religious ceremony in Greece and has often been described as the "Eleusinian Mysteries." The critic Benjamin Bickley Rogers has written a lucid note about this process: "The Chorus is represented as rehearsing

in the world below the early stages of that great annual procession from the Cerameicus to Eleusis in which they themselves, when alive, had been accustomed to participate. The Chorus must be supposed to have mustered in the great building provided for the marshalling of these and similar processions, and they are now calling Iacchus to come from the adjoining Temple of the Eleusinian deities and be their divine companion on the long twelve-mile journey. It was this torch-bearing Iacchus whom they escorted from the splendid temple where he dwelt at Athens along the Sacred Way to the sanctuary at Eleusis. The statue is brought out, all evil-doers are warned off, and then the procession commences, the Chorus singing hymns to each of the Eleusinian deities in turn, Persephone, Demeter, Iacchus, as they pass through the Cerameicus and out by the Eleusinian gate to the bridge over the Cephisus, where a little chaffing takes place, and whence they disappear from our sight on their way to the flower-enameled Thriasian plain."

(2) **The essential points of the dispute between Aeschylus and Euripides:** The three men, Dionysos/Euripides/Aeschylus, all make comments about drama. Here is a brief summary of their ideas.

Euripides on Aeschylus:
   (a) he is a charlatan, a boaster whose plays are brittle, overly structured.
   (b) his diction is primitive and makes no sense.
   (c) no one can understand his plays.
   (d) he is redundant.
   (e) his writing is unoriginal and dull.

Euripides on himself:
   (a) he inherited a flabby dramatic legacy from Aeschylus and cut away the bloat, interjected tickling phrases, prescribed gentle exercise and recommended a steady diet of gossip for everyone.
   (b) his plays represent true democratic Art where *everyone* speaks: women, slaves, kings, virgins, hags, etc.
   (c) he taught people how to speak by teaching semantics.
   (d) he brought real life to the stage, men and women just like those in the audience.

(e) the poet's chief duty is to speak truth for the improvement of the City.

Aeschylus on Euripides:
  (a) he cheapened theater by introducing characters of low breeding.
  (b) his plays poisoned the citizens by making them believe in a soft, undisciplined way of life.
  (c) Euripides and his 'Modernists' vilified themselves by infiltrating the theater with tawdry sexuality, vulgar obscenities, and so on.
  (d) he corrupted the decent wives of men by alluring them into a lifestyle of temptation.
  (e) Euripides taught bragging and silly gossip, thereby causing a shift from physical fitness to intellectual fancying.

Aeschylus on himself:
  (a) he created 'true' men in his plays, not sissies or degenerates.
  (b) his plays are patriotic, inspiring, and good for the morale of his audiences.
  (c) his philosophy states that a man's whole life must be given up to conquering his adversaries.
  (d) poetry/drama should be devoted to high themes, noble pursuits, and dignity.
  (e) poets exist in order to serve mankind.
  (f) the stage is no place for sexual encounters or "love-drooling"; it is the poet's duty to "conceal the filth. . . Let our concern be only with what's good."

Dionysos on Euripides and Aeschylus:
Dionysos serves more as a referee and instigator than as a commentator on theater. His statements are sometimes shrewd, sometimes corny. But his role is to bring out the competitiveness between the two playwrights and, ironically, to restore Aeschylus to a status above that of Euripides.

SUGGESTED ESSAY QUESTIONS

Long Essays:

1. What are the major causes of Athens' disintegration, according to Aristophanes? Include in your response the various political, social, and cultural forces at work.

2. Using two of Aristophanes' comedies, discuss the use of humor and wit, paying particular attention to such devices as double entendre and irony.

3. Write an essay on the role of women in Aristophanes' plays.

4. How does Aristophanes use symbolism as a dramatic technique?

5. "Aristophanes combines the grotesque with the sublime to bring about his vision of the universe." Discuss this statement with reference to at least two plays.

Short Essays:

1. Give two examples of a play on words, or puns, in Aristophanes' comedies and show how the author exploits the humor.

2. Why do you suppose Aristophanes' plays have lasted so long?

3. Would you consider Aristophanes a conservative or a liberal? Justify your response with references to the plays.

4. What is the role of religion in Aristophanes? How do the gods interplay with mankind?

5. It has been said that women are the stronger sex. Discuss the truth of this idea in reference to *Lysistrata*.

SELECTED BIBLIOGRAPHY

BIEBER, MARGARETE. *The History of the Greek and Roman Theatre.* Princeton, 1961.

BONNER, ROBERT J. AND GERTRUDE SMITH. *Justice From Homer to Aristotle*. Chicago, 1938.

CORNFORD, F. M. *The Origins of Attic Comedy*. Cambridge, 1914.

DEARDEN, C. W. *The Stage of Aristophanes*. London, 1976.

DOVER, K. J. *Aristophanic Comedy*. Berkeley, 1972.

EHRENBERG, VICTOR. *The People of Aristophanes: A Sociology of Old Attic Comedy*. Oxford: Blackwell, 1943.

ELDER, OLSON. *The Theory of Comedy*. Bloomington, 1968.

HENDERSON, JEFFREY. *The Maculate Muse*. New Haven, 1975.

LESKY, A. *A History of Greek Literature*. London, 1966.

LORD, LOUIS E. *Aristophanes: His Plays and His Influence*. New York: Cooper Square, 1963.

MCLEISH, KENNETH. *The Theatre of Aristophanes*. New York: Taplinger, 1980.

NORWOOD, GILBERT. *Greek Comedy*. New York, 1961.

PICKARD-CAMBRIDGE, SIR ARTHUR. *The Dramatic Festivals at Athens*. Oxford, 1968.

SPATZ, LOIS. *Aristophanes*. Boston: Twayne, 1978.

STRAUSS, LEO. *Socrates and Aristophanes*. Chicago: University of Chicago Press, 1980.

SUTTON, DANA FERRIN. *Self and Society in Aristophanes*. Washington: University Press of America, 1980.

USSHER, ROBERT GLENN. *Aristophanes*. Oxford: Glorendon, 1979.

WEBSTER, T. B. L. *Illustrations of Greek Drama*. London, 1971.

NOTES

NOTES

8/04 ∅ 4/96